Selecting Media for Instruction

Selecting Media for Instruction

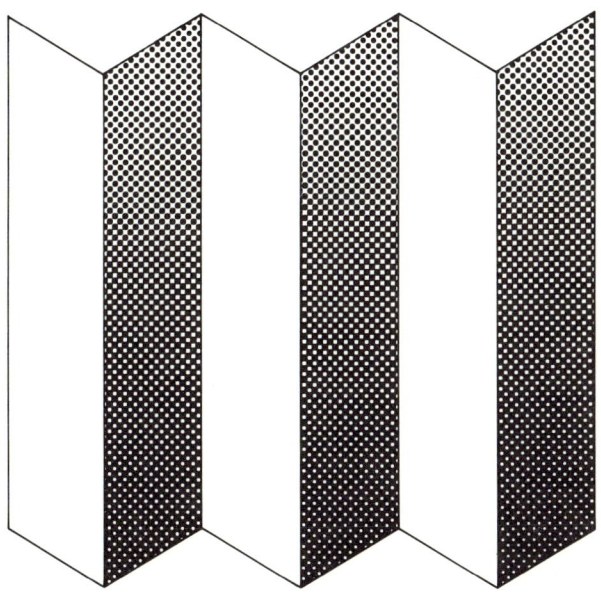

Robert A. Reiser and Robert M. Gagné
Florida State University

**Educational Technology Publications
Englewood Cliffs, New Jersey 07632**

Library of Congress Cataloging in Publication Data

Reiser, Robert A.
  Selecting media for instruction.

  Includes bibliographies and index.
  1. Teaching--Aids and devices. 2. Educational technology. I. Gagné, Robert Mills, 1916-
II. Title
LB1043.R43   1983   371.3'07'8   83-5686
ISBN 0-87778-187-7

Copyright © 1983 Educational Technology Publications, Inc., Englewood Cliffs, New Jersey 07632.

All rights reserved. No part of this book may be reproduced or transmitted, in any form or by any means, electronic or mechanical, including photocopying, recording, or by any information storage and retrieval system, without permission in writing from the Publisher.

Printed in the United States of America.

Library of Congress Catalog Card Number: 83-5686.

International Standard Book Number: 0-87778-187-7.

First Printing: June, 1983.

Table of Contents

Chapter 1: Introduction	3
Media in Instructional Design	5
Research on Media Effectiveness	6
What This Book Is About	7
Chapter 2: Some Characteristics of Media Selection Models	11
Format for Display of Media Selection Models	12
Categories of Media	13
Factors in Media Selection	14
Summary	26
Chapter 3: The Media Selection Model and Its Basis in Learning Research and Theory	31
The Media Selection Flowchart	31
Procedure Within a Chart	33
Basis for Model in Learning Research and Theory	36
Learning Outcomes	37
Events of Instruction	41
Learner Characteristics	43
Characteristics of the Model	44
Chapter 4: The Media and Their Uses in Instruction	49
Real Equipment and Simulators	49
Broadcast Television and Radio	51
Training Devices	53
Computers	54

Interactive Television	55
Sound Motion Picture and TV Cassette	56
Slide/Tape and Filmstrips	58
Charts and Training Aids	59
Slides and Overhead Projections	60
Printed Text and Programmed Text	61
Audio	62
The Instructor	63

Chapter 5: How to Use the Model 67
    What Is Needed 67
    How to Proceed 68
    The Flowchart Questions 70
    Final Selection Procedure 82

Chapter 6: Examples of the Model in Use 85
    Example 1—Broadcast Instruction, Adult Education 85
    Example 2—Self-Instruction, Science Education 88
    Example 3—Classroom Instruction, Vocational Education 94
    Example 4—Classroom Instruction, Sales Training 99
    Example 5—Self-Instruction, Military Training 102
    Summary and Conclusion 105

Chapter 7: The Model's Potential 107
    Evaluating the Model 107
    Ways of Using the Model 109
    What Benefits Does the Model Provide? 111
    Research Questions 114
    Concluding Statement 119

Index 123

Media Selection Flowchart .... Foldout

Selecting Media for Instruction

Chapter 1

Introduction

For a good many years, educators and trainers have faced the problem of choosing the appropriate media to deliver an instructional message. However important may be the personal contribution of teachers, instruction as a totality is bound to be composed of one or another type of media. Educators and trainers throughout the world spend a great deal of time and effort in attempting to choose appropriate media for particular instructional situations.

Many articles and books have been written about media for instruction and their selection. Some have described "systems" or "models" for media selection that are novel, while others have tried to synthesize the work that has been done in this field. There is, however, no generally accepted model. Most well-informed media specialists agree with Schramm (1977), who points out that no procedure can be applied automatically in every instructional situation. Guidelines for media selection, he says, must carefully consider local needs, situations, and resources.

Why should "selection of media" be a burning question? When does media selection become a critical issue? The answer is, of course, whenever instruction is being planned to be optimally effective. Much instruction is not planned that way, regardless of where and how it is delivered. But today's emphasis on effectiveness (including cost-effectiveness) and on accountability of instructional programs serves to make the role of media increasingly important to the total program. Instruction may take place in a school, college, or other form of learning center, and if the entire range of course offerings is considered, it is quite evident that the media possibilities range far beyond the filmstrip projector and the audio-cassette recorder. Much instruction is given to adult employees of business and industrial concerns. Such instruction, which is likely to be carefully planned, must give consideration to a variety of media, ranging from charts through film and TV to modified actual equipment. The television medium, and broadcast radio, are the preselected modes for delivery of a great variety of instruction to adults in their homes. What part might be played in this kind of instruction by simpler forms of media, such as printed checklists and workbooks? Trainers in business and industry must design instruction covering a great variety of job functions. So, naturally, designers of such instruction must be highly aware of the need for carefully made decisions about the choice of media. Some jobs deal almost entirely with paper; others are focused on transportable equipment; while still others require the operation of machines of great technological complexity. The desire to accomplish systematic instructional planning for such a variety of occupations brings to the fore the necessity of careful media selection.

Existing media selection models have a number of different origins and rationales. Some emphasize physical features of the various media, while others appear to concern themselves with categories of human sensing. In a recent review of media selection models, Clark and Angert (1981) arrive at the conclusion that available systems "reflect a preoccupation with technical considerations (e.g., convenience, portability) and are relatively short on instructional design considerations" (p. 13).

The model of media selection to be described here gives primary emphasis to instructional design factors, and proposes that these factors be given first consideration in a time sequence. The procedure involved focuses on the principles of human learning which affect decisions about media, to insure that the conditions favorable to learning are assured. Once these conditions are accounted for, practical factors—such as media cost and availability—can be taken into account.

Media in Instructional Design

The term "instructional media" has been defined in various ways. Some view media as hardware—the devices used to deliver instruction, such as motion picture projectors. Others equate media with the varieties of material, such as a filmstrip or printed text, that contain an instructional message. We define instructional media as *the physical means by which an instructional message is communicated*. Thus, by our definition, an instructor, a printed text, a slide/tape presentation, and the many other physical means by which an instructional message is communicated, are all considered media.

Selecting the appropriate medium is an integral step in the instructional design and development process. Almost all models for the design of instruction include a step requiring the selection of media. Most models indicate that media should not be selected until the specific events that will take place during an instructional sequence have been identified. In most models, media are then chosen, based in part on their ability to present the instructional events.

We assume that the various events that constitute an instructional sequence may be furnished more or less well, or more or less completely, by any given medium. For example, the feedback a student receives after performing a tennis backhand stroke may be more directly related to the student's performance if it is delivered via an instructor who observed the performance, as opposed to a videotape displaying what the performance should have looked like.

Since media differ in their ability to present the various events of instruction, the selection of media is likely to have a substantial influence on instructional effectiveness. Thus, in the tennis stroke example, had feedback been delivered via an instructor, student learning might have been greater than if feedback had been delivered via videotape. Logically, there should be a medium, or a group of media, best suited to delivering a particular instructional message. When that medium or media are employed to deliver the message, students should learn more than they would if other media were used. In a lesson designed to teach students the relation between force and acceleration, for example, it would seem that students would learn more if the lesson were taught using media that could depict motion than if media were employed that were not capable of showing motion.

Research on Media Effectiveness

For many years, investigators have attempted to identify those media best suited to teaching various instructional objectives. However, the research has not yet yielded results that permit definitive statements about the superiority of one medium over another in a particular situation (cf. Chu and Schramm, 1967; Schramm, 1977). In many of these studies, two media are used to present instruction, and the relative effectiveness of the two are compared. Often, students learn equally well from either medium.

The pattern of research results obtained may have come about for a variety of reasons. Some investigators incline to the belief that the research methodology employed has been faulty; either the wrong questions have been asked or the methods used to answer the questions have been inadequate. Others, however, tend to believe that the research findings reflect the actual situation; that is, it does not matter which medium you choose to teach a particular objective, almost any medium can do the job equally well. Gagné's statement that "most instructional functions can be performed by most media" (1970, p. 364) is occasionally cited as an example of this point of view. However, as Schramm (1977) points out, this statement in no way denies that in a given situation one medium may be more useful than others. Nor should it imply that attempts should not continue to be made to find the best combination of media for a given learning task. It is reasonable to suppose that for a given instructional task, and a given group of learners, various media will differ in terms of their instructional effectiveness. The media selection model described in this book is based on that premise.

What This Book Is About

This book is addressed to a variety of audiences. Its message is aimed primarily at instructional designers—those individuals in business and industry, governmental agencies, military services, and in education who design and develop instructional materials. Many of these individuals are regularly involved in selecting instructional media, but often do not employ a systematic means of arriving at a choice. For example, a recent survey of 29 instructional designers working at four United States Army schools revealed that only about ten percent of the designers used a systematic procedure when they were selecting instructional media (Reiser, 1981). Many of the designers who were interviewed indicated that certain portions of the media selection guidelines available to them were not specific enough, while other portions were too detailed. The media selection model to be described in this book is designed to overcome these problems.

In addition to its usefulness to instructional designers, the new model should also be of value to instructors and classroom teachers who select media for supplementing or supplanting some of their in-class teaching activities. Audio-visual specialists should find the model useful in aiding the evaluation and selection of non-print materials. The model may be expected to help administrators of instructional programs in making media selection decisions, as well as in judging the validity of media selection decisions made by others. Those involved in conducting media research and in teaching the research basis of instructional design should also find the book of interest, since it brings into focus many of the issues related to these areas.

The book is divided into seven chapters. This introductory chapter is followed by a chapter that presents a detailed review of some of the most prominent media selection models. This second chapter focuses on the physical and psychological factors incorporated in the various models, noting their common features and their differences.

In Chapter 3, a general description of our media selection model is presented. The chapter includes a discussion of the characteristics of the model and an account of the basis for the model in learning research and theory.

Chapter 4 reviews the various media included in the model. A description of the media characteristics which relate to learning effectiveness is presented.

Chapter 5 provides directions for using the model. A detailed description of each of the steps in the media selection process is included.

Chapter 6 provides a step-by-step description of how the model might be used in five different situations. Each situation involves a different instructional setting, different type of learning outcome, and different type of learner.

Chapter 7 describes how the model was evaluated, and explores potential applications of the model in public schools, universities, business and industry, and military training. Research questions related to the model are also presented.

As can be seen from the overview, the purpose of this book is not only to describe a new media selection model, but also to compare and contrast it with previous models, and to indicate the

Introduction 9

potential benefits of using the new model. We hope that after readers of the book perceive the advantages of the model, they will find it possible to use the model in their instructional design activities.

References

Chu, G.C., and Schramm, W. *Learning from television.* Washington, D.C.: National Association of Broadcasters, 1967.

Clark, F.E., and Angert, J.F. Teacher commitment to instructional design: The problem of media selection and use. *Educational Technology*, 1981, *21*(5), 9-15.

Gagné, R.M. *The conditions of learning* (2nd ed.). New York: Holt, Rinehart, and Winston, 1970.

Reiser, R.A. *A learning-based model for media selection: Development* (Research Product 81-25b). Alexandria, VA: Army Research Institute, 1981.

Schramm, W. *Big media, little media.* Beverly Hills, CA: Sage, 1977.

Chapter 2

Some Characteristics of Media Selection Models*

How should trainers and educators go about selecting media? A number of media selection models have been developed in an attempt to answer this question. Information concerning the usefulness of these models, however, is limited. It is rare to find detailed information about situations in which selection models have been employed.

Two studies have been identified in which media selection techniques were compared. In one instance, Braby (1973) compared the usefulness of ten media selection techniques. Models developed by Briggs (1970) and the Training Analysis and Evaluation Group (1972), as well as intuitive techniques, were judged superior to the seven other techniques. In another study, Romiszowski (1974) found that teacher trainees who used a media selection technique he developed made better media choices than did experienced teachers who used an intuitive approach.

In view of the limited empirical evidence regarding the relative merits of media selection models, the question of which model to employ cannot have a simple answer. An appropriate approach would seem to be to identify the features incorporated in the various models, decide which features are important, and select a model containing them.

---

*Portions of this chapter originally appeared in Reiser, R.A., and Gagné, R.M. Characteristics of media selection models. *Review of Educational Research*, 1982, 52, 499-512.

The purpose of this chapter is to identify and evaluate the relevance to learning effectiveness of the major features found in media selection models. Unlike previous reviews (e.g., Heidt, 1978; Levie, 1977), various models will not be described individually. Instead, the focus will be on the characteristics noted across models. The purpose of this approach is to invite attention to specific features as opposed to specific models. The features reviewed in this chapter include the physical forms the models take, the ways in which they classify media, and the media selection factors they consider. Our primary emphasis will be upon selection factors, because of their relation to the effectiveness of learning.

Nine models have been reviewed to yield the comparisons described here. Some of these models have become well-known over a period of years, while some have been recently reported. The models under consideration are cited as follows: Anderson (1976); Branson, Rayner, Cox, Furman, King, and Hannum (1975); Bretz (1971); Briggs and Wager (1981); Gagné and Briggs (1979); Gropper (1976); Kemp (1980); Romiszowski (1974); and Tosti and Ball (1969). In subsequent sections of this chapter, models will be identified by authors' names, omitting the date of the publication in which they are described.

Format for Display of Media Selection Models

The models under review present media features in flowcharts, matrices, or worksheets. An essential difference among these formats is the procedure for decision-making each demands. When a flowchart is used (e.g., Anderson; Bretz; Kemp; Romiszowski), the procedure leads to a progressive narrowing of media choices. Questions about media selection are posed in a particular order, and as each is answered, the number of candidate media is reduced. Typically, when the final question of the flowchart is answered, the designer is left with a small set of media from which to make a choice.

In contrast to the flowchart, the display of a matrix (e.g., Branson *et al.*) includes all the selection criteria at once. Using such considerations as the number of criteria met and their relative importance, the designer chooses from among the total set of media.

Worksheets present a kind of tabular array of media characteristics against desired criteria (e.g., Briggs and Wager; Gagné and Briggs). These also require that selection of media be deferred until all criteria have been considered. Presumably, worksheets could be used with a procedure requiring progressive narrowing of choices; but no such system has been proposed.

Although each of the three formats typically employed to display media selection models appears to be adequate, the flowchart format seems to hold one major advantage over the other two—it is usually simpler to use. Unlike worksheets, which often require fairly complex constructed responses, flowcharts only require the user to make selected responses, usually of the "yes-no" variety. And, unlike matrices and worksheets, which often require the user to weigh several factors simultaneously in order to arrive at a media choice, flowcharts allow the user to arrive at a final choice through a sequential process.

Categories of Media

A number of kinds of categories can be devised for the classification of media. Categories frequently employed include audio, print, still visual and motion visual, and real objects.

Reasons for using media categories are usually connected with the idea that a particular type of medium can best present a task having a similar classification. For example, the learning of a task which requires differentiation of visual features can best be done with a visual medium. Likewise, learning a task which depends upon receipt of an auditory message may best be accomplished with media which include audio. These are valid principles, included as well in those models which do not distinguish categories, but which attempt to assess the appropriateness of media for different instructional conditions (e.g., Briggs and Wager; Kemp).

While most media classifications depend upon characteristics of the display (visual, auditory, etc.), other dimensions have also been proposed. For example, Tosti and Ball suggest classification on the basis of (1) type of responses the media will accept, and (2) ways of adapting presentations to preceding learner responses. Gropper finds it desirable to categorize media according to their feedback capabilities, and also in terms of their ability to accommodate other events of instruction.

Factors in Media Selection

Instructors, classroom teachers, audio-visual specialists, trainers, and people whose job title may be "instructional designer" are likely to make use of media selection models. In succeeding portions of this book, we refer to all of them as "designers." The models to be described include a variety of factors to be considered by designers in selecting media. These factors fall into three categories: (a) physical attributes of media; (b) learner, setting, and task characteristics; and (c) practical factors.

Physical Attributes of Media

As indicated in Table 1, all of the models require the designer to consider the media attributes (i.e., physical capabilities of media) that are necessary in a given instance. For example, a designer may have to decide whether the medium to be employed in a particular instructional situation must be capable of depicting motion, although the conceptual basis for this decision may not be included.

Some Characteristics of Media Selection Models

Table 1

Factors Prominent in Various Media Selection Models

Factors	Anderson	Branson et al.	Bretz	Briggs and Wager	Gagné and Briggs	Gropper	Kemp	Romiszowski	Tosti and Ball
Learner, Setting, and Task Characteristics:									
Instructional Setting	X	X	X	X	X		X	X	
Learner Characteristics		X	X	X	X	X		X	
Categories of Learning Outcomes	X	X		X	X			X	X
Events of Instruction		X	X	X	X	X		X	X
Physical Attributes	X	X	X	X	X	X	X	X	X
Practical Factors		X	X	X	X	X	X	X	X

Note. An "X" indicates that the factor was prominent in a model. A blank space indicates that a model and its accompanying description either did not mention the factor or gave it little attention.

The models vary in the extent to which they stress direct consideration of media attributes. For instance, most of the questions included in Kemp's model require the designer to identify the media attributes that are appropriate (e.g., "audio-visual or multi-image technique necessary?"). In contrast, our model contains few questions concerning the media attributes necessary for a given instructional display. Instead, the designer is expected to attend to the characteristics of the intended learners, the instructional setting, and the learning task.

Visuals. All of the models require the designer to decide whether visual media are necessary. Some distinguish among various types of visuals (Branson *et al.*; Kemp; Tosti and Ball). For example, the ISD model (Branson *et al.*) requires the designer to choose between alpha-numeric, graphic, pictorial, and three-dimensional visual displays.

Visual media are frequently recommended to help students acquire certain concrete concepts, such as identifying objects (Anderson; Bretz; Romiszowski) and classifying spatial relationships (Bretz). Visual media are also considered useful in helping to teach students various motor skills. Bretz points out that words alone are usually an inefficient means of teaching a motor skill; visual demonstration is necessary.

Printed words. The requirement for presenting printed words is recognized by all of the models reviewed. The use of printed presentations is seen as a characteristic appropriate for learners who are good readers, as assessed by tested reading ability (Bretz), or as associated with increasing age (Gagné and Briggs).

Two of the models suggest that audio narration, as opposed to print, should be used with poor readers (Bretz; Briggs and Wager). There is some disagreement, however, as to whether audio narration is superior to print for affective objectives. Bretz states that audio may be superior, but Anderson indicates that print materials (including printed text, drawings, and photographs) are also appropriate for teaching affective objectives.

Other models indicate that if sound is not an integral part of the task to be learned, print may be appropriate (Anderson; Romiszowski). It is noted that print materials can be produced at a low cost (Branson *et al.*).

Sound. The capability of presenting sound is a media attribute included in several of the models. However, a distinction is sometimes drawn between verbal and non-verbal sounds (Branson *et al.*; Bretz; Gagné and Briggs; Kemp; Tosti and Ball). For example, Gagné and Briggs mention both verbal and non-verbal sounds, referring to them, respectively, as "spoken words" and "unusual sounds."

Sound media are considered necessary to present the appropriate stimulus information if the goal of instruction is the recall or recognition of sounds (Anderson; Bretz; Romiszowski). For example, Bretz points out that sound media are essential if the instructional goal is the appreciation of musical compositions or spoken poetry.

Another suggestion is that learner characteristics should be considered when deciding whether sound is necessary (Bretz; Briggs and Wager). Bretz states that since poor readers can understand spoken words more easily than written words, sound media should be used with these intended learners.

Motion. Pictorial motion is a media attribute included in many of the models. In some, specific distinctions about the type of motion are proposed. For example, the ISD model (Branson *et al.*) asks the designer to choose among still visuals, limited movement visuals, and full movement visuals. Somewhat similar motion types are identified by Kemp.

Generally, the reasons for considering the attribute of pictorial motion pertain to the need for depiction of human performance, and to the associated idea that learners will recognize or copy the movements shown (Anderson; Romiszowski). While asserting that motion is often unnecessary, Bretz lists three questions pertaining to the desirability of including motion. First, is the learning objective the performance of a procedure, the movements of which are unfamiliar to the learner? Second, is the learner required to learn a concept that is understandable only in terms of its "manner of movement"? And third, must the learner comprehend changes that take place too rapidly or too slowly to be identified, and which therefore require slow motion or fast motion displays?

Color. Only two of the models (Anderson; Branson *et al.*) require designers to decide whether the media to be selected must be capable of displaying colors. Anderson indicates that if the color of an object is relevant to the performance of some cognitive or psychomotor objective, a medium able to display colors should be chosen. A number of studies have indicated that the use of color in instructional materials will not result in increased learning unless color is directly relevant to what is being learned (Dwyer, 1978; Heidt, 1978; Schramm, 1972).

Real objects. Real objects, also known as *realia*, have been defined as "tangible objects, real items (as opposed to representations or models) as they are without alterations" (Association for Educational Communications and Technology, 1977, p. 293). Most of the media selection models reviewed require the designer to decide whether real objects should be used in a given instructional situation. Two models assert that real objects should be used to teach motor skills (Anderson; Romiszowski).

In addition to suggesting the use of real objects for teaching motor skills, Anderson indicates that, if practical, real objects may best be used to teach cognitive skills involving objects unfamiliar to the learner. Romiszowski makes a similar point. Neither author provides details of the reasons for using real objects in these situations. It seems evident that a training aid or device which reproduces the physical appearance of the real object may at least serve such an aim as familiarization.

The instructional setting is mentioned as another factor to be considered when deciding whether to use real objects. Briggs and Wager, as well as Kemp, indicate that real objects are appropriate for use in small groups and individualized instructional settings.

Leaders in the audio-visual field, like Dale (1969), have often stressed the benefits of using real objects and other media that present information in a "realistic" manner. However, this point of view has recently been called into question (Dwyer, 1978; Heinich, Molenda, and Russell, 1982; Salomon, 1981). Winn (1982) indicates that it is more important that information be represented in a manner that corresponds to the way learners represent information internally.

Learner, Setting, and Task Characteristics

The extent to which the models stress consideration of learner, setting, and task characteristics varies greatly. As indicated in Table 1, while each of the nine models requires consideration of at least one of the four factors we have grouped under the general heading of learner, setting, and task, only four of the models require direct consideration of all of these factors.

Instructional Setting. In Table 1, a model is classified as being concerned with instructional setting if it poses one or more of the following questions: In what location (e.g., school, home) is the instruction to be delivered? Is the instruction to be presented to individuals or to a group? If a group is to receive the instruction, what is the size of the group? Questions of this type are included in seven of the models.

Most of the models prescribe media for various settings and group sizes, but they rarely indicate why certain media have been recommended; only occasionally is a rationale provided. For example, one suggestion is that when instruction is delivered in an individualized mode, narration should be presented via print media, because print allows each learner to set his or her own pace, and thus allows for more efficient use of instructional time (Bretz).

Bretz also points out that individual instruction (as opposed to group) should be delivered via media capable of providing corrective feedback, so as to provide learners with information about the adequacy of their responses. He indicates that almost any medium can provide corrective feedback simply by stating the correct answer in such a way that the learner may compare it with his or her own.

Learner characteristics. In many media selection models, characteristics of the learner are considered important to the selection decision. Gagné and Briggs point out that many educators believe that media may be differentially effective for different types of learners, and that media should therefore be identified which are best suited to various learner types. Although researchers have had limited success in identifying the media most suitable for various types of learners (Bracht, 1970; Cronbach and Snow, 1977), several media selection models offer suggestions for selecting media on this basis.

Reading ability is one learner characteristic that is included in several media selection models (Branson *et al.*; Bretz; Briggs and Wager; Gagné and Briggs). In one of the models (Briggs and Wager), it is proposed that pictures can facilitate learning for those who are poor readers.

Another suggestion is that poor readers may benefit more from spoken words than from written ones (Bretz; Briggs and Wager). Bretz states that spoken words may be superior because poor readers can more easily understand them, especially if they are spoken in the learner's own idiom. However, he also points out that when good readers are working in a self-instructional mode, print materials provide greater pacing flexibility and therefore may offer a learning advantage over audio presentations. Briggs and Wager describe an advantage of print materials: print allows students to backtrack easily in order to review points that were previously missed.

Age is another learner characteristic often mentioned in media selection models (Briggs and Wager; Gagné and Briggs; Tosti and Ball). Older or more experienced learners may have developed learning strategies that enable them to manage some events of instruction for themselves. These learners, in contrast to younger or less experienced learners, may need to have fewer external instructional aids provided for them (Gagné and Briggs).

Two of the media selection models (Briggs and Wager; Gagné and Briggs) mention Dale's (1969) "Cone of Experience" as a tool that can be used to identify the appropriate media for a given age group. The Cone lists 12 categories of media and experiences in an ordered hierarchy. For cognitive objectives, it is suggested that it is efficient to use abstract media with older learners and concrete media and experiences with younger learners. For objectives involving attitude formations, Briggs and Wager suggest the opposite strategy; that is, abstract media are favored for use with younger learners, and concrete media and experiences for use with older learners.

Categories of learning outcomes. Classifying objectives in terms of the categories of learning they represent is an integral step in many media selection models. The number of categories included in the models reviewed ranged from three (Anderson) to eleven (Branson *et al.*). Most of the models include some or all of the categories of learning described by Gagné (1977)—intellectual skills, verbal information, motor skills, attitudes, and cognitive strategies. Specific media for various types of learning outcomes are prescribed by some formulations (Anderson; Branson *et al.*; Romiszowski). For example, Branson *et al.* suggest that when the desired learning outcome is an attitude, an instructor is often the preferred medium.

Similarities in several of the models (Branson *et al.*; Briggs and Wager; Gagné and Briggs; Gropper) are found in their suggestion of a procedure comprising the steps from the categorization of learning outcomes to the selection of media. This procedure entails categorizing learning outcomes, planning the instructional events to be used to teach each learning outcome, identifying the type of stimuli necessary to present those events, and finally, identifying the media capable of presenting those stimuli. The categorization of learning outcomes is a key step in this process; decisions regarding the instructional events to be included in a lesson are affected by the category of the learning outcome that is to be taught.

Events of instruction. The external events which support internal learning processes are called *events of instruction* by Gagné (1977) and Gagné and Briggs (1979). Most of the media selection models indicate that the events of instruction constituting a lesson should be planned before media to be used during the lesson are selected (Branson *et al.*; Briggs and Wager; Gagné and Briggs; Gropper; Romiszowski; Tosti and Ball). Media are then chosen, based in part on their ability to present the instructional events. Gagné and Briggs consider this approach to have a sounder rational basis than one which proceeds with the selection of media before instructional events have been planned.

A number of the media selection models provide guidelines intended to help designers choose appropriate media for presenting the various events of instruction. Two models (Briggs and Wager; Romiszowski) utilize charts indicating the degree to which particular media may be appropriate for presenting different instructional events. Other models include discussions of particular instructional events and the media most appropriate for presenting them.

The event called "informing the learner of the objectives" (Gagné and Briggs, 1979) is intended to provide learners with a clear indication of what they will be expected to learn, and thus to aid them in maintaining their orientation to the learning task and its expected outcome.

Bretz indicates that visual media, particularly those that can portray motion, may be the best choice for informing learners about objectives in the psychomotor or cognitive domains. He points out that these media can provide learners with an example of the skill they are expected to acquire; learners can use such an example as a model for judging their own performance during the instructional process.

Some Characteristics of Media Selection Models 23

The description of an objective may also serve the purpose of activating a motivational state in learners, by making clear to them what they will be able to accomplish once they have learned. Bretz indicates that this instructional function may best be served by those media capable of providing a vivid demonstration of the usefulness of the knowledge or skill described in an objective.

The purpose of the event "presenting the stimulus material" (Gagné and Briggs, 1979) is primarily to present learners with the stimuli (the "text") of the task to be learned. For example, if learners will be expected to state some verbal knowledge, that knowledge must be communicated to them. Or, if the learners will be required to identify items belonging to a certain class, they must be presented with examples of items belonging to that class. For tasks requiring identification of objects or symbols, the function of emphasizing distinctive features is included in this event.

Bretz makes the point that it is often best to have this event delivered by a medium other than a classroom instructor. In this view, the instructor's time can often be better spent in activities requiring a degree of human judgment and personal interaction, such as diagnosing learner problems.

The event called "eliciting the performance" (Gagné and Briggs, 1979) is an essential element in learning theory of any variety. By performing, learners practice what they have learned and thus set the stage for the occurrence of reinforcement.

Eliciting performance is discussed in many of the media selection models. Several indicate that the responses learners will be required to make should be categorized by type (e.g., overt, covert, motor, verbal, constructed, selected). According to this notion, the designer should attempt to select the media that are best able to elicit these particular types of responses (Gagné and Briggs; Gropper; Romiszowski; Tosti and Ball). Tosti and Ball also suggest that the designer should consider how frequently the responses will be required.

A rationale for considering response requirements when selecting media is presented by Gropper. He advocates a behavioral approach to instruction; practice of appropriate responses is the key element in such an approach. According to this notion, it is necessary first to identify the responses learners should be required to make, then to choose a means of eliciting those responses and to select the media that can best be used to accomplish this end.

The event described as "providing feedback" (Gagné and Briggs, 1979) involves providing learners with an indication of the degree to which their elicited performance has been correct. Usually, the intention is to give learners reinforcement.

Although two media selection models give prominence to this instructional event, the focus of their discussion varies greatly. One model suggests that learner characteristics should influence feedback and media selection decisions (Gropper). The other model suggests that almost any medium is adequate for presenting feedback (Bretz).

Gropper proposes that learner characteristics be considered when deciding upon the media to be used to present feedback. He indicates that error-prone learners may benefit from media that are able to incorporate remedial branches. He also suggests that anxious learners may require feedback that is designed to allay their anxiety; some media may be better suited than others to provide this type of feedback.

The event of "assessing performance" (Gagné and Briggs, 1979), often referred to as "testing," is intended to assess whether learners have acquired what they were expected to learn. Bretz points out that although print media are often used to assess learner performance, in certain instances, other media may be more appropriate. Printed tests assess learners' reading ability as well as their mastery of the skills being tested, and therefore the results of such tests can be misleading, especially if the learners are poor readers. Using audio-visual media to assess the performance of poor readers may be preferable in certain instances. In Bretz's view, audio-visual media are better able to assess learners' visual skills than are print media; in addition, they can be used to assess learner performance in more life-like situations.

Practical Factors

Practical factors such as media production costs and equipment availability must be considered during the media selection process, it is generally agreed. We believe, however, that practical criteria cannot be weighed in isolation. If practical factors were to dominate the media selection process, instruction of every sort would have chosen for it the most inexpensive and maintenance-free media, such as printed texts, audiotape voice recordings, or the diagrams made by an instructor on a chalkboard. Obviously, some kinds of instruction are helped by media which are a bit more complicated. For example, the printing of commercial posters is not learned from printed text, nor from an instructor's oral directions (although these may both be present); it requires a medium which displays models of print to the learner, and allows him or her to practice letter and word printing. The procedures of trouble-shooting a word processor are not likely to be adequately learned from voice recordings or printed texts—they too are helped by a medium which displays the electronic parts, circuits, or modules, and shows their functioning.

Although costs, availability, and convenience factors are of undoubted importance in the selection of media, that does not mean they should be the first to be decided upon. Quite the contrary procedure is likely to be best. First, consideration should be given to media which will help to insure the effectiveness of learning. When designers of instruction are satisfied that one or several media are appropriate for the desired instructional purpose, and that several other media are not, they can then confidently proceed to make decisions on the basis of practical considerations, with the knowledge that these decisions will not impair learning.

Most models propose that the consideration of practical factors can be done following a review of other factors, such as those described in the preceding sections. The practical factor most frequently mentioned is the cost of media, particularly production costs. Other factors often included are maintenance costs, hardware and software availability, instructor preferences, and production time.

Summary

In this chapter, most of the major features found in media selection models have been described. In some cases, a particular feature may be seen to be shared by all of the models reviewed; in other instances, features are unique to one or two. Differences among media selection models include the format used to display the models and the factors used in the selection process.

Selection of media is likely to be affected by a model's physical form of display. When a flowchart is employed, the process involves a progressive narrowing of media choices. However, when a matrix or worksheet is used, media choices are deferred until all selection criteria are examined. It appears to us that models which are displayed in flowchart form are easier to use. This is a particularly important consideration if many of those who will be using the model have had minimal experience in selecting media.

Decisions about media are also influenced by the selection factors included in a model. In several of the models reviewed, selection criteria focus on media attributes (i.e., the physical capabilities of media), such as the ability to present sounds or depict motion. Other models, however, focus on the characteristics of the intended learners, the instructional setting, and the learning task. We believe that proper identification of the media attributes necessary in a given situation is dependent upon consideration of the latter set of factors.

After questions about the learners, setting, and task have been addressed, the necessary media attributes can be readily defined and the media which possess those capabilities identified. The designer can then select from among those media on the basis of such practical factors as cost and availability.

In this chapter, we have reviewed the characteristics of current media selection models. In Chapter 3, we will describe the characteristics of our model and discuss the learning research and theory upon which the model is based.

References

Anderson, R.H. *Selecting and developing media for instruction.* New York: Van Nostrand Reinhold, 1976.

Association for Educational Communications and Technology. *Educational technology: Definition and glossary of terms.* Washington, D.C.: AECT, 1977.

Braby, R. *An evaluation of ten techniques for choosing instructional media* (TAEG Report No. 8). Orlando, FL: Training Analysis and Evaluation Group, 1973.

Bracht, G.H. Experimental factors related to aptitude-treatment interactions. *Review of Educational Research,* 1970, *40,* 627-647.

Branson, R.K., Rayner, G.T., Cox, J.L., Furman, J.P., King, F.J., and Hannum, W.H. *Interservice procedures for instructional systems development* (5 vols.) (TRADOC Pam 350-30). Ft. Monroe, VA: U.S. Army Training and Doctrine Command, August 1975.

Bretz, R. *The selection of appropriate communication media for instruction: A guide for designers of Air Force technical training programs.* Santa Monica, CA: Rand, 1971.

Briggs, L.J. *Handbook of procedures for the design of instruction.* Pittsburgh: American Institutes for Research, 1970.

Briggs, L.J., and Wager, W.W. *Handbook of procedures for the design of instruction* (2nd ed.). Englewood Cliffs, NJ: Educational Technology Publications, 1981.

Cronbach, L.J., and Snow, R.E. *Aptitudes and instructional methods.* New York: Irvington, 1977.

Dale, E.A. *Audiovisual methods in teaching* (3rd ed.). New York: Holt, Rinehart, and Winston, 1969.

Dwyer, F.M. *Strategies for improving visual learning: A handbook for the effective selection, design, and use of visualized materials.* State College, PA: Learning Services, 1978.

Gagné, R.M. *The conditions of learning* (3rd ed.). New York: Holt, Rinehart, and Winston, 1977.

Gagné, R.M., and Briggs, L.J. *Principles of instructional design* (2nd ed.). New York: Holt, Rinehart, and Winston, 1979.

Gropper, G.L. A behavioral perspective on media selection. *AV Communication Review,* 1976, *24,* 157-186.

Heidt, E.U. *Instructional media and the individual learner.* London: Kogan Page, 1978.

Heinich, R., Molenda, M., and Russell, J.D. *Instructional media and the new technologies of instruction.* New York: John Wiley, 1982.

Kemp, J.E. *Planning and producing audiovisual materials* (4th ed.). New York: Harper and Row, 1980.

Levie, W.H. Models for media selection. *NSPI Journal,* 1977, *16*(7), 4-7.

Romiszowski, A.J. *The selection and use of instructional media.* London: Kogan Page, 1974.

Salomon, G. *Communication and education: Social and psychological interactions.* Beverly Hills, CA: Sage, 1981.

Schramm, W. What the research says. In W. Schramm (Ed.), *Quality in instructional television.* Honolulu: University Press of Hawaii, 1972.

Tosti, D.T., and Ball, J.R. A behavioral approach to instructional design and media selection. *AV Communication Review,* 1969, *17,* 5-25.

Training Analysis and Evaluation Group. *Staff study on cost and training effectiveness of proposed training systems* (TAEG Report No. 1). Orlando, FL: Training Analysis and Evaluation Group, 1972.

Winn, W. Visualization in learning and instruction: A cognitive approach. *Educational Communication and Technology Journal*, 1982, *30*, 3-35.

Chapter 3

The Media Selection Model and Its Basis in Learning Research and Theory

The model described in this volume takes the form of a flowchart containing six panels, each representing a different instructional situation. Each panel begins with a list of candidate media. These are the media which remain as possible choices; that is, they have not been eliminated by the flowchart procedure of previous panels.

Beginning with these candidate media in mind, the instructional designer follows the procedure by answering successive questions, arriving at a much smaller set of media on the "bottom line" of the chart. Subsequent choices among these are made by considering the practical factors of cost, availability, and convenience.

Determining media appropriateness, and thus narrowing the process of media selection, takes only a few minutes with the use of the flowchart. By working through the flow-diagram, the instructional designer can be assured that no important factor of potential aid to human learning has been neglected. The media selection process can then proceed with the confidence that such factors have been taken into account.

The Media Selection Flowchart

The flowchart (presented in full foldout format at the back of this volume) presents an unfolding series of charts, six in all. Each chart represents a set of decisions within a general area of conditions of the instructional system, such as "C. Self-Instruction with Readers," or "F. Instructor with Non-Readers." The charts are arranged in sequence so that those decisions having the most important implications for the instructional system are made first. The first chart ("Chart A. Job Competence Decision") pertains to the choice of real equipment (either large or portable) or a simulator as a necessary medium of instruction; obviously, these items usually entail a large expense.

The decisions governing the choice of which of the six charts will receive primary attention are actually "instructional situation" decisions. If it has been determined that students are widely dispersed, a broadcast system may be desirable, and the appropriate chart selected as a starting point. Alternatively, it may have been decided that students can best be served by an individualized mode of instruction rather than by an instructor-led class. Again, the appropriate panel of the flowchart is sought. The panels of the flowchart are as follows:

A. Job Competence Decision.
B. Central Broadcast Decision.
C. Self-Instruction with Readers.
D. Self-Instruction with Non-Readers.
E. Instructor with Readers.
F. Instructor with Non-Readers.

Still another set of determinations need to have been made prior to using the flowchart, and this is simply the identification of objectives and their classification into five types (Gagné, 1977). Any particular course is likely to include many specific instructional objectives. The procedure of media selection may best be utilized when media requirements are considered for a clustered set of objectives, all of which belong to the same domain of learning outcomes (intellectual skills, verbal knowledge, cognitive strategies, motor skills, attitudes). For example, a course for nurses may include objectives which pertain to the operation of three different pieces of equipment. For each piece of equipment, there are likely to be objectives which fall into the category of intellectual skills. The decision whether to cluster the total set of course objectives in this fashion should be made by the instructional designer, based on his or her experience with the goals for which instruction is being planned. It should be noted that dealing with groups of objectives falling into a single domain of learning outcome should not lead to a neglect of other domains. The objectives related to the operating of three different pieces of equipment are likely to have in common, besides intellectual skills, some aspects of safety belonging to the domain of attitudes. The existence of several types of learning outcomes needs to be constantly borne in mind by the designer as he or she proceeds to identify appropriate media within the confines of each chart.

Procedure Within a Chart

The prior decision about the instructional situation will make possible the rapid progression to a chart such as "C. Self-Instruction with Readers." In this progression, certain media have been successively eliminated from consideration, so that each chart begins with a somewhat different set of candidate media. Chart C, for example, omits such media as broadcast radio and TV; Figure 1 reproduces Chart C.

The decision process within each chart begins with a question contained in a numbered diamond-shaped box. The question shown within the diamond is actually an abbreviated form of the question having the same number, listed at the bottom of the chart. Thus, Chart C begins with the two questions, "7. Self-Instruction?" and "8. Readers?," and proceeds to question "9. Either an Attitude or Verbal Information?" Answering this question "yes" sends the designer to another diamond-shaped box, 11, which asks, "Attitude? Does the instruction aim to influence the

34 *Selecting Media for Instruction*

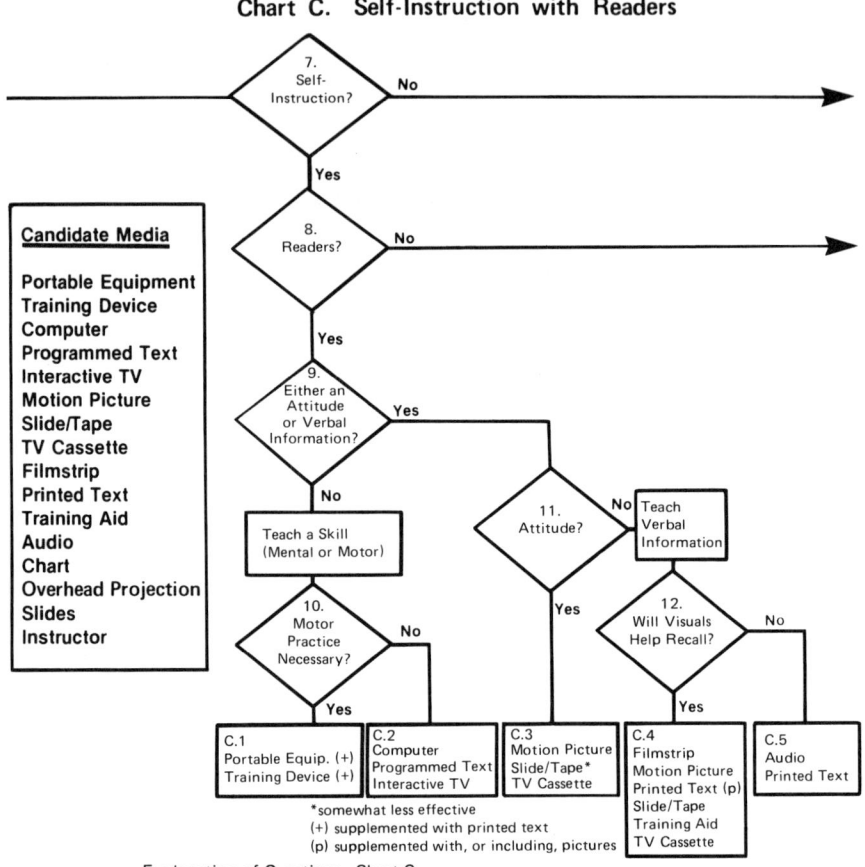

Figure 1. Flowchart panel applicable to the instructional situation "self-instruction with readers."

student's values or opinions?" Should this question be answered "yes," the designer is led to a box at the bottom of the diagram indicating that desirable choices of media are a motion picture, TV cassette, or the less effective slide/tape combination.

Returning to a consideration of decision 9, should the answer here be "no," then the designer has chosen to proceed to teach an intellectual (mental) or a motor skill, and must now proceed to distinguish these two kinds. Diamond-shaped box 10 asks, "Motor Practice Necessary?" This is the case, of course, if a motor skill is the objective. If the answer to 10 is "yes," a bottom-line box shows that appropriate media may now be reduced to two: portable equipment and training device (either supplemented with a printed text).

Now, at the right-hand side of the chart, if the answer to "11. Attitude?" is "no," this means that verbal knowledge must be taught. Diamond-shaped box 12 poses the final question as to whether visuals will help the recall of verbal knowledge. Six different media are possible if the answer is "yes." If visuals will not aid recall, audio or printed text remain as desirable media for these self-instructing students who are readers.

The process is continued until a decision leads to the identification of a set of media, each of which is capable of aiding the learning of the task or tasks to be learned. In the charts, this set of media is brought down to a rectangular box which is the "bottom-line" box. Sometimes, as many as ten media may be in this box, or as few as one. For example, in Chart C applying to Readers, six media are listed in the bottom-line box following a "yes" answer to question "12. Will Visuals Help Recall?" In contrast, in Chart D applying to Non-Readers, a "yes" answer to the same question leads to a bottom-line box listing three media. Quite evidently, what have been excluded in going from Chart C to Chart D are media utilizing printed messages.

In general, the media in each bottom-line box are considered to be about equally appropriate for support of the type of learning outcome which has been identified by the decisions leading up to that box. Obviously, they differ in other respects, such as cost or availability, and considerations of this sort must now be applied in order to arrive at a final media choice.

Basis for Model in Learning Research and Theory

The primary source depended upon as a basis for rational derivation of the present model is systematic knowledge of human learning as revealed by scientific research and theory. Many recently published volumes provide descriptions of cognitive learning theory. Prominent among these is a series of handbooks edited by Estes (1975, 1976, 1978a); in addition are volumes by Anderson (1980) and by Bower and Hilgard (1981). Instructional principles based upon the general model of learning processes involved in these theories are described by Gagné (1977) and by Gagné and Briggs (1979). Although these latter works are not intended to be the sole references for such principles, they nevertheless must be frequently cited as being most directly relevant to the media selection model.

The choice of learning theory as a basis for rational derivation of the model obviously means that other groundings have been rejected. While it is evident that several other characteristics of media cannot be ignored, they do not appear to have been successful as bases for the generation of positive media selection procedures. This includes such a variety of categories pertaining to media attributes as mode of sensory stimulation (Romiszowski, 1974), physical nature of stimulation (Bretz, 1971), type of learning experience (Dale, 1969), function with respect to the learner (Tosti and Ball, 1969), or some combination of these (Anderson, 1976; Kemp, 1980).

The principles of learning involved in the derivation of the media selection model are of two main sorts. First, they embody distinctions among categories of what is learned. It is supposed that learned entities make possible the exhibition of several different categories of performance by the learner. Thus, when they have completed their learning, human learners have acquired lasting *capabilities* to carry out certain performances (Gagné, 1977). These categories of performance represent *learning outcomes*, and may conveniently be spoken of in these terms. A second set of learning principles pertains to the external events which stimulate the learner and which, according to theory, perform the function of supporting internal learning processes. These occasions of stimulation are referred to as *events of instruction* (Gagné, 1977; Gagné and Briggs, 1979). Which of these events a given medium is best able to provide is a matter of direct relevance to media selection.

Learning Outcomes

The five kinds of learning outcomes distinguished by Gagné (1977) and Gagné and Briggs (1979) imply the need for different instructional treatments, some of which are best provided by one group of media, some by another.

Intellectual (mental) skills are capabilities that enable the learner to deal with his or her environment symbolically, as he or she does in using language or mathematics. These skills include all entities known as *concepts*, whether these are "concrete" (as in the identification of classes of objects or object qualities) or "abstract" (as in identifying a bus line, or a bank). And, most importantly, they include *rules* ("relationships"), which, as their name implies, relate concepts to each other. There are rules of language, such as how to make subject and verb agree, or where to place topic sentences in paragraphs. There are many rules of arithmetic, algebra, and geometry, such as the rule that vertical angles are equal. There are rules of science, such as Newton's Laws and Archimedes' Principle. Learned capabilities like these are exhibited when the learner shows he or she can apply them to any new concrete instance.

Intellectual skills may be exemplified by simple mathematical operations, for instance, identifying quarters as fractional parts of a whole. In presenting this related set of rules (four quarters equal a whole, two quarters equal a half, etc.), visuals can perform several learning support functions, to be described in a subsequent section. However, the most important characteristic of intellectual skills learning, so far as media are concerned, is its requirement for *precise corrective feedback*. Instruction must be so arranged that the learners make responses (such as "½") which can be followed by feedback that communicates precisely "correct," "incorrect," or "correct in a specified part." Thus, regardless of what other media characteristics are being employed, the overriding requirement in teaching intellectual skills is for *interactive* operation, as provided, for example, by programmed instruction or by computer-based instruction. When display media such as radio or TV are employed, interactive operation may be attained by using supplementary workbooks or other printed materials. It is notable that such materials formed an integral part of a project which successfully taught arithmetic by radio (Searle, Friend, and Suppes, 1976).

Verbal information forms the largest part of most instruction. For example, training in conservation of the physical environment consists of knowledge about geographic features of the land, soil, water, rivers, forests, animals and their habits, the growth of crops, and many related matters. When learners acquire organized knowledge of this sort, the kind of performance they are expected to exhibit is one of stating the knowledge in such a way as to convey its essential meaning. This sort of performance implies the restatement of general ideas, sometimes called *schemata* (Bransford, 1979), but not the recall of specific facts in verbatim form. Since verbal knowledge is exhibited in this relatively imprecise form, it is possible also for the feedback for correct performance to be similarly imprecise. That is to say, for verbal knowledge, feedback needs to contain a message such as "you have the right general idea," rather than "you are exactly correct."

The relaxation of the need for feedback precision makes possible the use of a wider range of media for verbal knowledge than is the case for intellectual skills. Feedback which does not need to be precise can be delivered in a number of ways by media which do not possess true interactive properties. For example, after first encouraging viewers to try saying the major causes of motor vehicle accidents, a TV or movie presentation can then assure them, "If you mentioned drunkenness and speeding, these are two of the main causes. Others are (A) and (B)." Such feedback may be presumed to be reasonably effective for verbal knowledge learning even though it (a) has a non-specific form, and (b) bears no precise relation to the responses actually made by individual viewers. Feedback of this imprecise sort is, as previously noted, ineffective for the learning of intellectual skills, and this is the basis for differential media requirements.

Cognitive strategies of "learning to learn" and problem-solving may be acquired and practiced by way of media presentations. A number of strategies have been described as aids to learning and remembering (O'Neil, 1978). When practice in problem-solving is the aim of instruction, although the acquiring of new cognitive strategies may be intended, intellectual skills (rules, concepts) are normally involved in arriving at problem solutions. For this reason, the main requirement on media is the provision of precise feedback following learner performance. Media having interactive properties are therefore required. The presentation of simulations via the computer is a frequently employed use of a medium possessing this characteristic.

A fourth kind of learning outcome, *motor skills*, can be aided substantially in initial stages of learning by media presentations which permit the learner to imitate the procedure. In effect, the procedure, sometimes called an "executive subroutine" (Fitts and

Posner, 1967), is an intellectual skill; consequently, requirements for feedback precision are the same as those previously described for that type of outcome. Once the basic procedure is learned, improvement in the smoothness and timing of motor skills depends upon direct practice of the movements themselves. For such improvement, kinesthetic feedback from the involved muscles is essential; somehow, the learner must practice the movements that comprise the actual performance. Accordingly, what is needed as a medium is the "real situation" (as in driving), the real equipment (as an electric can-opener), or a realistic simulator (as for hovering a helicopter).

The fifth type of learning outcome, *attitude*, is often readily established or altered with the help of media. Attitudes are learned internal states that influence choices of personal action. Examples are attitudes of "choosing a career in law," "choosing golf as a participant sport," or "choosing to avoid harmful drugs." Thus, the presence of an attitude is not inferred from the learner's performance itself, but rather from the choices he or she makes of actions of which he or she is capable. According to one prominent line of theory (Bandura, 1969), attitudes are most readily established through the agency of a *human model*. The choices communicated by the human model are imitated by the learner, and vicariously reinforced. The model may be an actual human being, or an animate figure who exhibits human characteristics (e.g., Smokey the Bear, Snoopy). The essential media characteristic for attitude learning is the display of a human model in the process of making the desired choices, and the model's satisfaction with the consequences of those choices. Evidently, this requires the display of human action, and this in turn implies a preference for those media which show movement. The advantages of television for the purpose of establishing or changing attitudes are immediately obvious.

Events of Instruction

Another major theoretical strand providing a basis for the media selection model consists of the successive steps in external stimulation of the learner that support internal processes of learning. These steps are called events of instruction, and according to Gagné and Briggs (1979), they occur in the following approximate order:

(1) gaining attention;
(2) informing the learner of the objective;
(3) stimulating recall of prerequisite learning;
(4) presenting the stimulus material;
(5) providing "learning guidance";
(6) eliciting the performance;
(7) providing corrective feedback;
(8) assessing the performance; and
(9) enhancing retention and transfer.

As Gagné (1974, 1977) has shown, these events can be rationally derived from the general model of cognitive learning theory. Thus, for example, "stimulating recall of prerequisite learning" translates directly into cognitive learning theory as "retrieval of prior learning to working memory"; "providing 'learning guidance' " has the meaning in terms of cognitive theory of "suggesting the semantic encoding of information."

While all nine of these events are considered to comprise instruction, they do not all have differential implications for media selection. For example, event number 2, "informing the learner of the objective," may be made to happen in a variety of ways depending on the medium being employed, but so far as is known, these ways do not differentially influence learning effectiveness. In contrast, event number 7, "providing corrective feedback," requires that media possess certain characteristics (interactive ones) if the event is to occur at all. Particular consideration must be given to some of these external events, but not to each one, as reflected in the characteristics of media.

Presenting the stimulus material is an event that must on some occasions be given particular attention in media selection. These instances arise when the learning objective requires the differentiation of features of the task situation. For example, teaching someone to read an electric meter requires instruction that includes a representation of the physical features of the material object, whether by means of a training aid, a simulated meter, or a real meter. The instruction may be guided by other kinds of stimulation, including verbal directions, but it must include the perceptual learning that enables the learner to *distinguish features* of the task. Since many practically useful human performances involve visual perception, learning to selectively perceive the features of such tasks frequently requires the use of visual presentations. Similarly, when the features to be distinguished are auditory, as in the learning of foreign languages, audio-based media become appropriate.

Learning guidance is provided in a number of ways designed to enhance the semantic encoding process which, according to theory, enables the storage of what is learned in long-term memory (Bower, 1975). Media often provide outstanding opportunities for multiple encoding, as well as for enormous variety in the presentation of associated ideas ("elaboration"). Visual media, in particular, make possible the display of pictures to activate visual images and thus take advantage of the superior retentivity of multiple encoding (Paivio, 1971). In addition, visual media such as the videodisc permit a varied mosaic of words, symbols, and pictures to be presented within a short time interval. The enhancement of semantic encoding is one of the most obviously supportive functions that can be accomplished by media. It occurs whenever media are able to supplement terse language communication with various forms of message elaboration.

The twin events of *eliciting the performance* and *providing corrective feedback* are essential elements in cognitive learning theory, as they have been in virtually all theories of learning. The key concept governing the importance of these events is *reinforcement*, the feedback of information to the learner concerning the probable rewarding or punishing outcomes of action (Estes, 1978b). Providing corrective feedback of this sort requires that the learner be able to respond to an instructional presentation, and that information then be given to the learner regarding the correctness (or degree of correctness) of his or her response. Media possessing these characteristics are called *interactive*.

The event described as *enhancing retention and transfer* is, in a sense, simply an extension of the idea of semantic encoding. Continuing to provide message elaboration improves the possibility of multiple encoding. Not only during original learning, but also in subsequent periods of spaced review (Gagné, 1977), this event is likely to be readily accomplished by media, particularly those having visual displays. Of singular importance may be instruction which uses pictures to suggest images, since these can provide the learner with an added source of *cues for retrieval* of what has been learned.

Learner Characteristics

Another set of factors underlying the development of the media selection model is the characteristics of learners. These factors have both theoretical and practical origins in their relation to the processes of learning.

Amount of experience as a learner is likely to determine the presence of accumulated knowledge, and also of cognitive strategies which enhance the processes of learning and remembering. Thus, more experienced learners may be expected to exercise greater control over the events of instruction than is the case with learners of lesser experience. For more experienced learners, some of the events of instruction may be presented in abbreviated form or omitted entirely. In the extreme, this trend leads to the employment of self-instruction, which requires the selection of appropriate media having features that make corrective feedback possible.

Ability to read, that is, to gain information from printed text, is an important individual ability from both the theoretical and practical point of view. If facile reading of text cannot be accomplished by the intended students of a program of instruction, those media displaying printed messages (books, computers) would best be excluded as possibilities. It is important to consider whether students can, with reasonable efficiency, gain information from printed text. The identification of students as readers or non-readers serves as one of the major divisions in our media selection model.

What about the kinds of characteristics that give students particular affinities for learning from certain media? The set of "mental skills" (Olson and Bruner, 1974; Salomon, 1974) that may be developed in learners as a result of specialized practice with motion picture film and TV presentations can presumably become stable characteristics of the learner. Salomon's (1979) work shows that media may be employed to cultivate learner abilities attuned to the various symbol systems embodied in media presentations. The implication of these studies is that enhanced learner characteristics, particularly in the area of visualization, may be developed by appropriate design of media-based training. Learner characteristics of this sort, when they are the objectives of instruction, are readily handled by the present model.

Characteristics of the Model

The model being described here takes a concrete form as a flowchart for use in the job of instructional design, as an aid to the task of selecting media. The flowchart enables the designer, within the framework of a known instructional situation, to engage in a process of progressive exclusion of media, and thus to arrive at a relatively small set of "final candidate media," which are appropriate for the particular instruction being planned. This small set can then be further tested against practical criteria of cost, availability, and convenience.

According to the present model, the primary set of factors to be given initial consideration in making media choices is that set which influences learning effectiveness. The identification of these factors has been based upon modern theory and research in human learning. The following set of learning factors are among those which have been accorded prominence in deriving the model:

(1) the instructional situation, whether classroom with instructor, student self-instruction, or other;
(2) the scope of the segment of instruction for which media are to be chosen;
(3) the objectives of the instruction;
(4) the domains of outcomes intended to be accomplished by the learning; and
(5) certain critical events of instruction.

In use, the flowchart provides a convenient and relatively rapid way of reducing decisions about media to a manageable number. The designer is encouraged to employ a natural, sequential mode of thinking, as opposed to one which requires the simultaneous judging and weighing of a number of features of differing degrees of importance. It is expected, therefore, that instructional designers will find the flowchart a job aid which they are well prepared to use, and which they welcome as a distinct help to the task of media selection. By employing the flowchart, designers will be able to arrive at media decisions which carry the assurance that factors favorable to learning have been taken into account. With this kind of presumption, the designer can proceed to select media on the basis of such practical factors as cost and availability, unimpeded by doubts about instructional effectiveness.

References

Anderson, R.H. *Selecting and developing media for instruction.* New York: Van Nostrand Reinhold Company, 1976.

Anderson, J.R. *Cognitive psychology and its implications.* San Francisco: Freeman, 1980.

Bandura, A. *Principles of behavior modification.* New York: Holt, Rinehart, and Winston, 1969.

Bower, G.H. Cognitive psychology: An introduction. In W.K. Estes (Ed.), *Handbook of learning and cognitive processes, Vol. 1.* Hillsdale, NJ: Erlbaum, 1975.

Bower, G.H., and Hilgard, E.J. *Theories of learning* (5th ed.). Englewood Cliffs, NJ: Prentice-Hall, 1981.

Bransford, J.D. *Human cognition.* Belmont, CA: Wadsworth, 1979.

Bretz, R. *The selection of appropriate communication media for instruction: A guide for designers of Air Force technical training programs* (R-601-PR). Santa Monica, CA: The Rand Corporation, February 1971.

Dale, E.A. *Audiovisual methods in teaching* (3rd ed.). New York: Holt, Rinehart, and Winston, 1969.

Estes, W.K. (Ed.) *Handbook of learning and cognitive processes, Vol. 1: Introduction to concepts and issues.* Hillsdale, NJ: Erlbaum, 1975.

Estes, W.K. *Handbook of learning and cognitive processes, Vol. 4: Attention and memory.* Hillsdale, NJ: Erlbaum, 1976.

Estes, W.K. *Handbook of learning and cognitive processes, Vol. 5: Human information processing.* Hillsdale, NJ: Erlbaum, 1978(a).

Estes, W.K. *On the organization and core concepts of learning theory and cognitive psychology.* In W.K. Estes (Ed.), *Handbook of learning and cognitive processes, Vol. 6.* Hillsdale, NJ: Erlbaum, 1978(b).

Fitts, P.M., and Posner, M.I. *Human performance.* Monterey, CA: Brooks/Cole, 1967.

Gagné, R.M. *Essentials of learning for instruction.* New York: Holt, Rinehart, and Winston, 1974.

Gagné, R.M. *The conditions of learning* (3rd ed.). New York: Holt, Rinehart, and Winston, 1977.

Gagné, R.M., and Briggs, L.J. *Principles of instructional design* (2nd ed.). New York: Holt, Rinehart, and Winston, 1979.

Kemp, J.E. *Planning and producing audiovisual materials* (4th ed.). New York: Harper & Row, 1980.

Olson, D.R., and Bruner, J.S. Learning through experience and learning through media. In D.R. Olson (Ed.), *Media and symbols: The forms of expression, communication, and education. The Yearbook of the National Society for the Study of Education.* Chicago: The University of Chicago Press, 1974.

O'Neil, H.F., Jr. (Ed.) *Learning strategies.* New York: Academic Press, 1978.

Paivio, A. *Imagery and verbal processes.* New York: Holt, Rinehart, and Winston, 1971.

Romiszowski, A.J. *The selection and use of instructional media: A systems approach.* London: Kogan Page, 1974.

Salomon, G. What is learned and how it is taught: The interaction between media, message, task, and learner. In D.R. Olson (Ed.), *Media and symbols: The forms of expression, communication, and education. The Yearbook of the National Society for the Study of Education.* Chicago: The University of Chicago Press, 1974.

Salomon, G. *Interaction of media, cognition, and learning.* San Francisco: Jossey-Bass, 1979.

Searle, B., Friend, J., and Suppes, P. *The radio mathematics project: Nicaragua 1974-1975.* Stanford, CA: Institute for Mathematical Studies in the Social Sciences, Stanford University, 1976.

Tosti, D.T., and Ball, J.R. A behavioral approach to instructional design and media selection. *AV Communication Review*, 1969, *17*, 5-25.

Chapter 4

The Media and Their Uses in Instruction

The kinds of media encompassed by our selection model range from the simplest to the most complex. At the simple end of this dimension, we list a *chart*, which may actually take the form of writing or drawing on a chalkboard. At the complex end, the media are *simulators* and *large (non-portable) equipment*. Viewed as hardware, the range of media is about as great as it can be along the simple-complex dimension. The appropriateness of a medium, and its usefulness for instruction, however, are not related in any direct way to its complexity or size as hardware. It will, therefore, be informative to consider the characteristics of various media which relate to learning effectiveness. The order in which individual media are discussed generally reflects the order in which they are listed as candidates for selection in the flowchart, as described in the next chapter.

Real Equipment and Simulators

Real equipment, either large or portable, is used in training when certain activities which are part of the job must be well practiced and free of error. Critical performances in driving a truck are examples. A medium or device which simply represents the appearance of the equipment cannot insure transfer of training to the job with sufficiently high probability. The managers of training must feel confident that essential activities will be performed in an error-free manner. If errors occur, they are likely to endanger the operations of equipment, or the health and well-being of other people. Accordingly, Chart A of our model, which deals with the selection of this kind of equipment, asks the question, "Are the consequences of task error serious?"

Using real equipment for training is an expensive course of action, particularly when the equipment is large. The decision may be simplified when the equipment is small, portable, and, therefore, not very expensive. Thus, one would scarcely hesitate to use a real food blender as a medium for the training of a kitchen worker, or a real rifle for the training of a soldier.

Besides real equipment, simulators may also be employed when error-free performance is desired. The simulators used in the training of commercial airplane pilots, and for the training of helicopter pilots, are highly complex machines which reproduce the operating characteristics of the real equipment with high fidelity. Although expensive in themselves, simulators nevertheless usually cost less than the real equipment, and this reduced cost is one factor leading to their selection as media. A second important reason for this choice, though, is that the conditions required for training may be impossible to achieve in any way other than by simulation. Thus, the pilots of space vehicles spend much time practicing their procedures in simulators prior to their actual flight in space. Pilots of commercial aircraft practice in simulators the procedures for various emergency conditions of flight—emergencies which cannot be made to occur in a real airborne craft without endangering life.

The argument in favor of simulation may be extended somewhat when the situation for which training is given does not involve large equipment, but instead consists of complex decision-making. Simulation in this sense is employed in such exercises as strategic defense games, war games, air traffic control, and business games. School instruction often includes consumer games, career games, and the like. The resemblance of these types of simulation to the equipment simulator lies in the estimation that learning transfer from training to the job situation is likely to be very high; that is, errors, particularly gross errors, will be entirely avoided.

From the standpoint of instructional outcomes, training must sometimes be designed to produce performances whose probability of error is exceedingly low. This error-free quality may be expected even for the first time the task is performed, without any on-the-job practice. The consequences of error in certain jobs (e.g., aircraft pilot, truck driver, equipment operator, air traffic controller) are perceived as being dangerous to the point of threatening injury or loss of life. When such conditions prevail, it is clear that the choice of media needs to be "real equipment" or "simulation of real equipment."

Broadcast Television and Radio

Broadcasts of television and radio are employed as media when the potential students are widely dispersed, and when it is possible for them to receive instruction at scheduled times. As the less expensive of the two, radio broadcast has been used for many years in locations where people's residences are separated by great distances (e.g., countries of South America, and Australia). With the advent of satellite transmission, TV broadcasting of educational programs has grown in frequency. Large systems of adult education using TV broadcast have been developed by such organizations as the Open University of Great Britain and the University of Mid-America.

In general, radio and TV broadcast have demonstrated effectiveness in conveying useful knowledge to widely dispersed populations of people (Schramm, 1977). When intellectual skills, such as arithmetic, foreign language, or the like, are to be taught, some special features must be built into the programs. Such features, in general, are designed to elicit responses from the learner. The techniques of *Sesame Street* (Lesser, 1974), for example, establish a responding routine for the characters shown in the program. Children tend to imitate these responses, and are thus "drawn in" to participation. Similar techniques may be used in adult programs. However, these ways of effecting interaction between the learner and the medium are not perfect; interaction, after all, is merely encouraged, not required.

Learners may be required to respond to radio and TV broadcasts when the latter are part of courses which require answers to printed questions contained in supplementary materials. For the learning of intellectual skills, the combination of broadcast program and printed booklets which are an integral part of each lesson, and which require learner responses, can be highly effective. A successful example of teaching mathematics by radio (in Nicaragua) employed this kind of combination (Searle, Friend, and Suppes, 1976). An example using television broadcast is described by Mayo, Hornik, and McAnany (1976).

Radio and TV broadcasts may be the media of choice when verbal information is to be conveyed, as in accounts of history, current events, or practical items like dates, names, and locations. Secondly, because they can establish attitudes by showing the choices made by human models, TV broadcasts are particularly appropriate for this kind of instructional objective. As for a third possibility, when skills are to be taught, whether motor (such as using tools) or intellectual (as in multiplying square roots of numbers), broadcast radio and TV lack essential provisions for response reception and feedback. For the learning of such skills, broadcast media work best when they are made "interactive." Typically, this is done by using accompanying workbooks or response sheets in printed form. Combinations of broadcast and supplementary printed sheets for the recording of student responses have been found to be highly effective for the learning of intellectual skills. In another mode of use, an instructor may provide feedback for student responses to broadcast instruction.

Training Devices

Although a familiar type of medium in many kinds of training situations, the meaning of the name "training device" has probably been longest understood by the military services. A training device, strictly speaking, is not a simulator, because by design it makes no attempt to reproduce the operating characteristics of the real equipment. For this reason, a training device can be a great deal less expensive than either the real equipment or a simulator. What the training device does attempt to do is to provide training of component skills in an interactive manner. That is to say, the training device receives learner responses and gives appropriate feedback to them. By so doing, it becomes a highly effective medium for the training of critical skills.

An example of a training device is a maintenance trainer for some complex electronic equipment (for example, a cathode ray tube, a high-fidelity amplifier). A training device of this sort may be constructed so as to lay out on a panel the major critical circuits of the electronic equipment. Malfunctions may be introduced so as to require circuit checking and tracing to find the troubles. This kind of item is obviously a device which provides for learner response and feedback. It is not a simulator, since its design has made no attempt to represent the operational equipment (the electronic device) with fidelity. As a training device, it is performing its assigned role as a medium well adapted for training.

Another example of a training device is an automobile driver trainer, whose purpose may be to provide the learner with practice in making proper choices of controls (braking, steering, or both), appropriate choices of direction (right, left, forward), and rapid reactions to unexpected events. Obviously, in order to do this, the training device must faithfully represent certain aspects of the driving situation, such as the relation of steering to turning, the relation of braking to deceleration, the appearance of the "road ahead," and the like. Yet, a driver trainer, in its most common form, makes no attempt to simulate the operating characteristics (including the "feel") of an automobile. Were it to do that, it would indeed become a simulator, and would be very expensive to manufacture.

Skills are the targeted training aims of training devices. The latter may be used to train component motor skills, such as those involved in automobile driving. Even more frequently, they may be successfully employed in the training of intellectual skills, for example, those involved in tracing malfunctions in electronic circuits. Training devices teach skills because they are "interactive media"; in other words, because they receive the learner's responses and provide feedback to them. At the same time, it is evident that they would be needlessly complex and expensive for the teaching of verbal knowledge, and minimally effective for use in establishing attitudes.

Computers

The typical conformation of the computer as a medium for learning consists of a display screen coupled to a set of control disks or tapes, and responded to by the learner via a typewriter keyboard. In microcomputer form, which now is highly popular and widespread, this combination of devices is fairly affordable to a great many households, as well as to schools. The kinds of displays possible are letters and numerals alone or in connected discourse, and a variety of graphics representing real and imagined objects in two dimensions. Some computers are also able to deliver audio information and instructions. Response modes possible to the computer include typing, pointing, and drawing. Speaking is also likely to become a common response mode, perhaps by using a coded or standardized language.

The computer is an interactive medium. It is, therefore, of particular usefulness for instruction in intellectual skills—language skills, numerical skills, geometric skills, and spatial skills. Almost without a second thought, it is the learning of intellectual skills that even the novice instructional designer tries to accomplish with a "courseware" program designed for the computer. And so we have a great many instructional programs to teach the skills involved in reading, spelling, and writing; as well as those in arithmetic, algebra, geometry, trigonometry, and in subjects of science such as mechanics and the strength of chemical solutions. It may be noted that these common topics for computer-based instructional programs are skills of the intellectual variety, not the motor kind. The latter are possible to training devices; some kinds of motor skills of eye-hand coordination may be practiced on the computer, such as the target aiming of various video games, but the variety as yet appears limited.

The computer appears to be a medium well adapted for instruction in intellectual skills. Not only can such complex equipment provide the accurate feedback necessary for initial skill learning, it can also continue to present to the learner a succession of examples, and thus make possible extensive and varied practice (Atkinson, 1968; Suppes and Morningstar, 1969).

Interactive Television

The display features of computers may be vastly enhanced when they are coupled with television. This may be done using a TV tape cassette. However, the full potential of the combination may be realized with the videodisc. The latter method of recording and playing back the video signal has the property of fast random access to particular display segments, thus providing the flexibility and speed of feedback that are most desirable when intellectual skills are to be learned.

The computer-videodisc combination, then, possesses the characteristic of permitting "interactive" use (without supplementary materials), essential for the learning of intellectual skills. The great versatility of this combination stems from the fact that desirable properties of the sound and motion display of TV are also present. Thus, the great advantages of the sound and picture combination for the teaching of verbal knowledge, and the human action possibilities for the communication of attitudes, are all present in this one medium. The interactive property, added to the already powerful characteristics of the sound motion picture (TV), makes the videodisc-computer a combination capable of assuring effectiveness for a great variety of learning goals.

Sound Motion Picture and TV Cassette

The learning possibilities of the sound motion picture medium are considerable, as attested by the widespread use of sound films and videocassettes in programs of education and training. It is generally recognized that the motion picture and the video picture with sound are essentially equivalent so far as their effects on learning are concerned.

What special properties make the sound motion picture such a useful medium? For what kinds of learning outcomes is this medium (either film or TV) most useful? There are three parts to the answer. First, pictures accompanied by sound may constitute a very effective way of emphasizing distinctive features for those tasks which require distinguishing the visual aspects of stimulation. For example, teaching learners to complete a complicated printed business form may be done well when particular entry categories are given emphasis by pictorial means (circling, zooming) and also simultaneously by sound (oral reading of the category). This kind of media treatment aids the learner in learning to make distinctions among those features to which he or she must learn to respond differentially.

The second reason for employment of the sound motion picture (film or TV) with advantage is the ability of this medium to convey verbal information in ways which provide immediate "elaboration" of that information. The sound motion picture does not simply state a fact by oral speech; it also shows that fact, illustrates it, and within a few moments, puts it in a larger context of knowledge related to the fact. These various kinds of elaboration, via sound track and picture, increase the memorability of the basic statement. Even when the learner's attention occasionally and momentarily wanders, he or she is surrounded by a complex of information which buttresses the main idea being conveyed by that small segment of the display. As recent research indicates (Nugent, 1982), the duplication of sensory channels, and more specifically, the richness of elaborated information, are features that contribute to ease of learning and also to the strength of retention of verbal information.

The third valuable property of the sound motion picture combination is its ability to show human beings and their actions. The feeling of reality, of "being there," by the viewers of such programs (heightened, usually, by the big screen) is a well-recognized experience. The educational uses of depicting human beings in action primarily center around the establishment or modification of attitudes. Sound films designed to modify attitudes in such areas as avoidance of harmful drugs, keeping a clean environment, establishing good work habits, and the like, are well known. Such films are more effective when they employ "human models" in the manner suggested by the work of Bandura (1969).

To summarize, the sound motion picture has advantages as a medium for aiding the learning of distinctive features of tasks, for the teaching of verbal information, and for the establishment of attitudes. This combination is, then, a medium both flexible and highly versatile. There is little reason to wonder at its popularity, nor at the prominent place it holds within the realm of useful media.

Slide/Tape and Filmstrips

Both the slide/tape medium and filmstrips possess the capability of displaying still pictures, usually in a predetermined order, accompanied by sound (usually oral speech). The properties of these media which relate to learning effectiveness may perhaps be best considered as diminished characteristics of the sound motion picture, as previously described. The sound itself may be essentially similar, whether delivered by sound track or by the instructor's voice. Since the pictures are not moving, however, they are diminished in their ability to provide as many distinctive cues, to surround the statements of verbal information with as rich a network of elaborative scenes, and in their ability to display the high degree of realism in human models and their activities.

The slide/tape and filmstrip with sound perform many of the same functions as does the sound motion picture. These functions are (a) the provision of cues to distinctiveness in visual tasks; (b) the elaboration of verbal information; and (c) the depiction of human models and their actions in the modification of attitudes. Of course, these media are much less expensive than the sound motion picture (film or tape). Do the former media do as good a job, or a job that is "good enough"? In many situations, they do. Deciding to use these simpler media obviously involves decisions about costs, as well as considerations of the nature of the learners, their age, educational status, and their estimated motivational states.

Either the slides or the filmstrip may be used without a pre-recorded sound track. In that case, essentially the same effect may be obtained from the accompanying voice of an instructor. Naturally enough, the content of what the instructor says may make the greatest difference as far as student learning is concerned.

Charts and Training Aids

A frequently used medium, usually as part of an instructor's presentation, is a chart or chalkboard diagram. These media are of great usefulness in illustrating relationships among objects or events, or relationships of parts to wholes. Diagrams may illustrate, for example, ordered parts of an organization or system, the flow of operations in an industrial process, the circulation of blood in the body, or the theoretical arrangement of atomic particles. Generally speaking, spatial relations in diagrams, and also the shapes of figures, are made to "stand for" other kinds of relations which are inherently abstract, such as "precedes in time," "contributes to," "causes," and so forth. By so doing, they serve as concrete organizers of concepts to be learned, and also provide retrievable cues to the remembering of these concepts. When the diagram to be presented is stable, and unlikely to require modifications, an instructor may make use of charts on cardboard, hardboard, or other stock, which may contain specially prepared versions of the objects to be displayed. In this configuration, a chart may take the form of a *training aid*, a category which includes surface layouts, models, and mockups that provide displays of parts and processes of a system on which instruction is being given.

Whether in the form of chalkboard drawing, paper surface with large print, or manufactured training aid, the chart is particularly useful to give emphasis to distinctive visual features, and also to show (by analogy) relationships among concepts of the subject being taught. These forms of media, then, are particularly well adapted to aid the learning of intellectual skills (concepts and rules). When employed for this purpose, the demands of effective learning would add the requirement that the instructor make systematic provisions for student performance and for the subsequent feedback to that performance.

Slides and Overhead Projections

Projected slides and transparencies constitute a highly flexible media category having many uses. These media can be used to show drawn diagrams possessing the properties described in the previous section on Charts and Training Aids. They are able to present drawings which help the learner to differentiate objects on the basis of their distinctive visual features. They are also capable of displaying diagrams which illustrate relations among concepts, and by that means conveying the meanings of more abstract concepts and rules. These potentialities are common to all media which make use of visual displays.

Projected slides are able to perform other valuable functions. They may show actual photographs of objects, people, or scenes. Such representations of reality are of obvious usefulness when such things as the distinctive features of paintings, or the distinctive features of an abdominal cavity in an appendix operation, are being studied and learned. Photographed pictures are also useful in connection with the teaching of other kinds of learning outcomes, such as verbal information; when knowledge of historical events is being taught by an instructor, slides which can show the events in pictorial form are of aid in the learning and later retrieval of that information. When the flow of change in architectural styles is the subject of instruction, photographic slides would appear to be an essential accompaniment to an instructor's lecture; the requirement is for distinctive features embedded in a context of historical events.

Slides containing photographs of people can presumably be employed to display human models, and thus to contribute to the learning or modification of attitudes. Obviously, though, the absence of motion depicting actions of these human models places some limitations on their effectiveness. Realism and credibility of the model may be limited when shown only in still photographs. As was true of the slide/tape medium and filmstrips with sound, the absence of motion in these soundless media diminishes their effectiveness in predictable ways.

When used by an instructor to teach concepts or to convey verbal information, slides can make distinct contributions to learning effectiveness. In this kind of employment, both small slides and transparencies are highly versatile media. Typically, they play the part of aids to an instructor who assures that learner responses and feedback are made to be an integral part of instruction.

Printed Text and Programmed Text

Surely no medium is as widely employed as the printed text, whether in the form of loose typewritten sheets, workbooks, or the closely printed pages of textbooks. For conveying verbal information, it is impossible to find a more efficient medium than the printed text, provided that the learners are proficient as readers. When such conditions prevail, the learning of verbal information from text is probably several times as rapid as with the use of any other medium. For facile readers, too, evidence indicates that learning is often more effective from printed text than from other media, including those containing pictures (Briggs, Campeau, Gagné, and May, 1965).

The effectiveness of print as a medium is not confined to verbal information. Concepts and rules (intellectual skills) may readily be learned from printed texts by competent readers. Of course, good learning conditions for skills also require learner performance and feedback. These can be provided in print form in workbooks containing blanks, or in *programmed texts*. A printed text has a programmed form when it requires frequent responses and provides feedback to them.

Since the learners who participate in many training situations do not read well, the effectiveness and efficiency of print is often surpassed by media which have the capability of visual display. As previous sections have indicated, media such as slides, slide/tapes, and motion pictures are able to teach intellectual skills and verbal information even to learners who are poor readers.

Audio

Recorded oral instruction is capable of bringing about learning of verbal information, guiding the learning of intellectual and motor skills, and even establishing attitudes, under some circumstances. The communication (and subsequent learning) of facts, names, dates, legends, and other organized knowledge has been accomplished by oral speech as long as human beings have been able to talk. While this means is somewhat diminished when speech is recorded rather than delivered face-to-face, our long experience with broadcast radio and with tape-recorded speech leaves no doubt of the general effectiveness of this medium.

Audiocassette tapes are widely employed to teach occupational concepts and skills, such as office procedures, insurance marketing, and many others. Tapes are used by physicians, lawyers, and other professionals to keep abreast of the latest developments in their technical fields. In more formal educational settings, intellectual skills may best be taught when audiotapes are supplemented with printed materials or workbooks that make provisions for student responding and corrective feedback.

Audio sound tracks or tapes are unlikely to have much effect on attitudes by virtue solely of the message they contain. However, the introduction of a respected and admired human model whose voice is recognized by listeners can be highly effective for attitude change. Dramatic programs, like the radio shows of a previous age, would undoubtedly be successful in affecting attitudes, were the listeners to become familiar with, and "attached to," the characters portrayed. From broadcast radio of the 1930s, many examples of attitude change could be cited, including those resulting from the "fireside chats" of President Roosevelt. While audiotapes are not widely used for this purpose, their potentiality is nevertheless apparent.

The Instructor

An instructor may manage the presentation of instruction in a great variety of ways, and in doing so may choose from among a considerable variety of media—slide/tape combinations, films, training aids, printed texts, or any others in a large set of "candidate media." When functioning in this manner, the instructor is an instructional manager, one of whose tasks is to select appropriate media for the objectives to be attained. It is our hope that this book will help instructors perform this "instructional management" aspect of their jobs.

For certain objectives, instructors may on occasion decide to "do it themselves"—in other words, to deliver by means of oral speech the content to be learned and also the guiding "directions" which tell the learner what and how to learn. It is possible, then, to view this narrowly defined instructor function as a medium. A definition of the instructor acting as a medium might be: "personally delivered face-to-face oral speech." Depending upon the type and number of learners, the mode of teaching may be tutoring, small-group instruction, or lecturing; a discussion of these varieties goes beyond the scope of this volume (see Gage, 1976).

Personally delivered oral speech may unquestionably be employed to effect learning of verbal information. Although basically similar to recorded speech, personally delivered speech may succeed better in communication since the instructor can adapt his or her delivery to listeners' reactions (alertness, attentiveness, signs of misunderstanding, etc.). Much of the content of the typical lecture is verbal information, with an organization suggested or imposed by the lecturer.

As previously noted, oral speech can guide the learning of intellectual skills—concepts and rules. Experienced learners are able to acquire intellectual skills from hearing oral presentation, probably because they are able to put into effect the necessary performance-feedback events by themselves. Younger and less sophisticated learners, however, are likely to learn much less from an instructor's lecture itself, so far as the attainment of new intellectual skills is concerned. For such learners, a teaching mode partaking more of tutoring is required, with provision for questioning and individualized feedback to student responses.

Naturally enough, the medium of "personally delivered face-to-face oral speech" is a favorable vehicle for the formation and modification of attitudes. When attitudinal objectives are considered an important part of instruction, the instructor may be chosen as a medium primarily in order to optimize attitude learning. Should this be a choice made for any given training situation, it is essential to bear in mind that the instructor will be, in performing this function, a human model. For attitudinal instruction to be effective, the human model must be perceived as admirable, credible, and powerful (Bandura, 1969; Gagné, 1977). These requirements, of course, imply that the instructor must be selected as possessing appropriate qualities, in addition to being capable of delivering understandable oral speech.

References

Atkinson, R.C. Computerized instruction and the learning process. *American Psychologist*, 1968, *23*, 225-239.

Bandura, A. *Principles of behavior modification*. New York: Holt, Rinehart, and Winston, 1969.

Briggs, L.J., Campeau, P.L., Gagné, R.M., and May, M.A.

Instructional media: a procedure for the design of multi-media instruction, a critical review of research and suggestions for future research. Palo Alto, CA: American Institutes for Research, 1965.

Gage, N.L. (Ed.) *The psychology of teaching methods. Seventy-Fifth Yearbook of the National Society for the Study of Education, Part I.* Chicago: University of Chicago Press, 1976.

Gagné, R.M. *The conditions of learning* (3rd ed.). New York: Holt, Rinehart, and Winston, 1977.

Lesser, G.S. *Children and television.* New York: Random House, 1974.

Mayo, J.K., Hornik, R.C., and McAnany, E.G. *Educational reform with television: The El Salvador experience.* Stanford, CA: Stanford University Press, 1976.

Nugent, G.C. Pictures, audio, and print: Symbolic representation and effect on learning. *Educational Communication and Technology Journal*, 1982, *30*, 163-174.

Schramm, W. *Big media, little media.* Beverly Hills, CA: Sage, 1977.

Searle, B., Friend, J., and Suppes, P. *The radio mathematics project: Nicaragua 1974-1975.* Stanford, CA: Institute for Mathematical Studies in the Social Sciences, Stanford University, 1976.

Suppes, P., and Morningstar, M. Computer-assisted instruction. *Science*, 1969, *166*, 343-350.

Chapter 5

How to Use the Model

This chapter presents the six charts that constitute our media selection model and provides directions for using it (the full six-panel foldout flowchart is found at the back of this book). A description is given of the information a designer must have prior to using the model. A detailed explanation of each of the questions contained in the flowchart is also provided. Finally, a procedure for making a final media selection decision is outlined.

What Is Needed

As the previous chapters have indicated, a number of different factors must be considered when instructional media are being selected. In order to use the media selection flowchart presented in this book, an instructional designer needs to have information about several features of the intended instruction. A designer will be able to proceed rapidly through the flowchart if this information is gathered beforehand. The information that should be gathered includes:
 (1) the objectives to be taught;
 (2) the domain of learning outcome to which each objective belongs (i.e., intellectual skill, verbal information, cognitive strategy, motor skill, or attitude);
 (3) the setting in which the instruction will take place (e.g., will the instruction be broadcast from a central location? Will

the instruction be delivered by a live instructor? Will the students be expected to learn by self-instruction?); and

(4) whether or not the learners are expected to be competent readers (i.e., whether they are able, with reasonable efficiency, to gain information from printed text).

Prior to use of the flowchart, selection should be made of suitable *scope* of instruction for which media are being selected. An entire course is likely to be too large a segment because its variety of learning outcomes may be too great for consistent treatment. On the other hand, applying the flowchart procedure to a single learning event is likely to be an inefficient process. The flowchart may best be utilized when considering the media requirements for an objective or a clustered set of objectives which are part of the same lesson or module, and which belong to the same domain of learning outcomes.

How to Proceed

In order to maintain a record of choices for later use, the designer should list each objective or set of objectives for the lesson or module on a Media Selection Worksheet (Figure 2). Copies of the blank worksheet should be made so that it can be used on a repeated basis. With an objective or set of objectives in mind, the designer then proceeds through the flowchart, beginning at Chart A. Unless an arrow indicates otherwise, the general direction for advancing through the chart is to the right and down. When a box on the bottom line of the flowchart is reached, each of the media listed there is to be indicated by a check mark on the Media Selection Worksheet. Media are listed on the worksheet in alphabetical order. The worksheet will be used later during the final selection procedure.

How to Use the Model

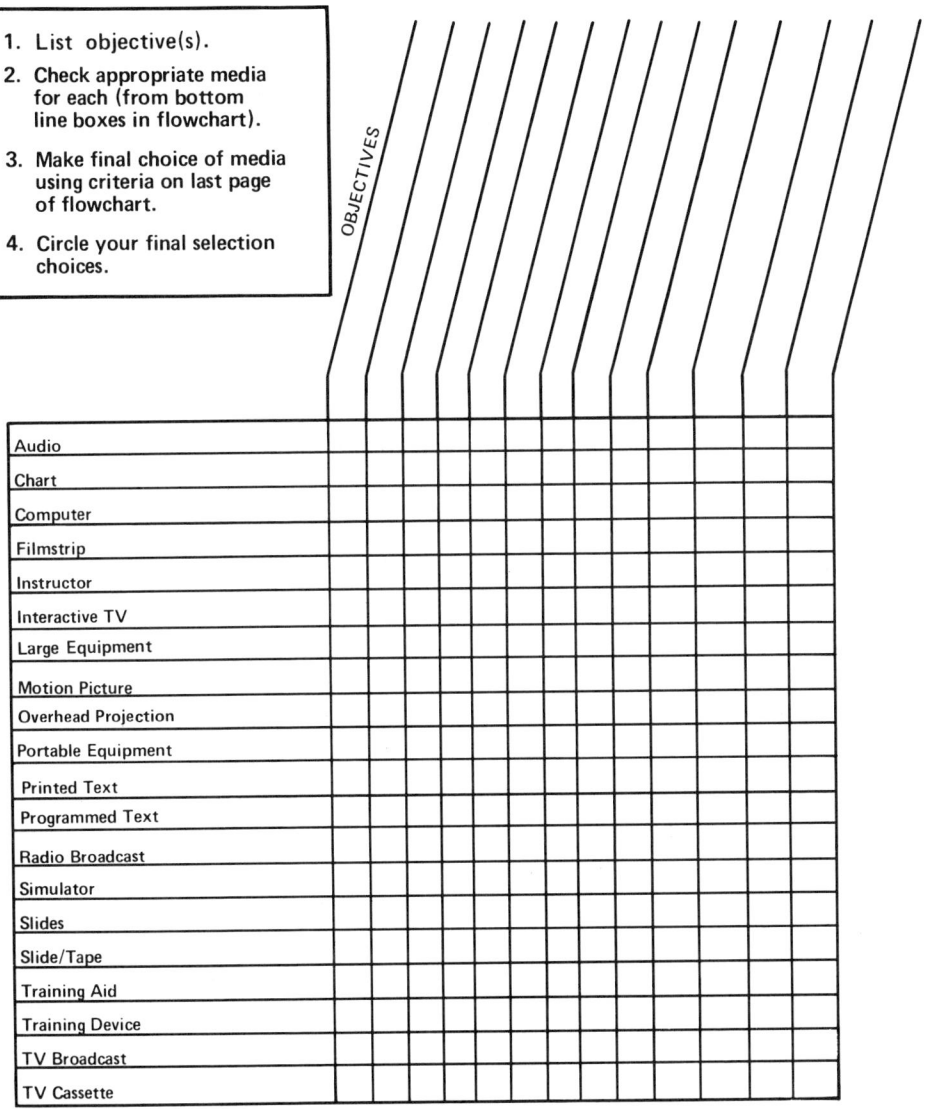

Figure 2. The Media Selection Worksheet.

The Flowchart Questions

Each chart of the media selection flowchart includes a series of numbered questions, designed to identify with increasing specificity the nature of the instructional situation in which media will be employed. As each question is answered, the instructional situation becomes more clearly defined, and the number of media appropriate for that situation is accordingly reduced. The following sections provide detailed explanations of the flowchart questions within each chart.

Chart A. Job Competence Decision

Chart A is shown in Figure 3. This chart consists of a single question designed to ascertain the importance of performing the task without error at the end of the designated training period.

Question 1. Consequences of Task Error Serious? Are there serious consequences of error when the student is first required to perform the task outside of the instructional setting? Does the instruction which is planned include the requirement that, at its end, the student will perform the task without error? For example, in the job of a nurse, one expects a task such as using a blood pressure cuff to be brought to a mastery (no-error) level by the time the period of instruction is completed. In contrast, an error in the performance of a clerk, while undesirable, has a low probability of being serious in the sense of directly endangering people. Furthermore, errors in many clerical tasks can be corrected by supervisors and are expected to decrease in frequency as job experience is gained.

When error in a task is considered to have serious consequences, it is reasonable to conclude that students will require "direct practice" on these tasks. Thus, a "yes" answer

How to Use the Model

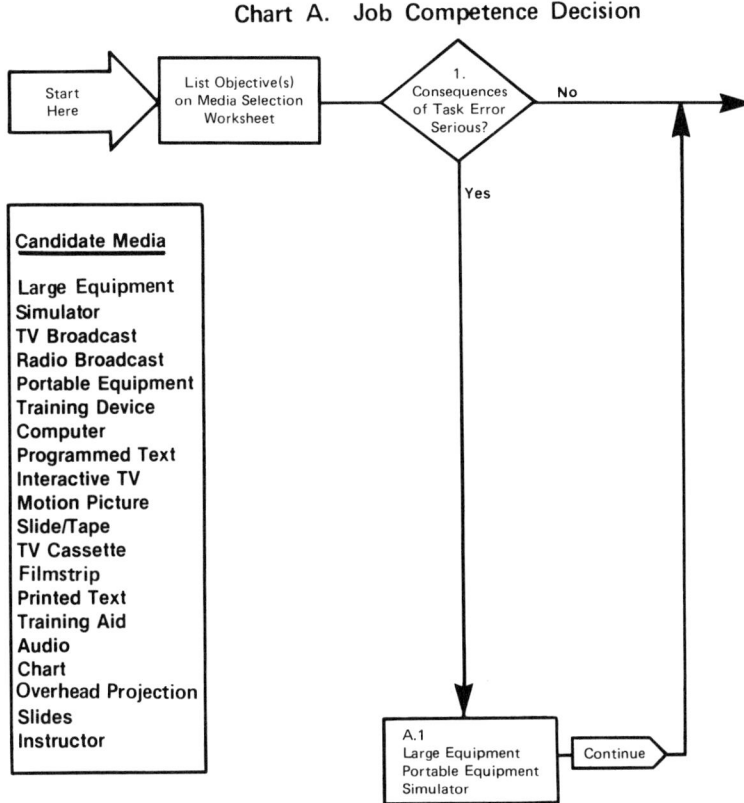

Figure 3. Flowchart panel pertaining to the "job competence decision."

to this question leads to the selection of either the real object (large or portable) involved in performance of the task, or a highly realistic simulator.

If a real object or a simulator is selected at this point, the designer should nevertheless proceed through the rest of the flowchart in order to consider additional media which may aid in other phases of instruction, including other classes of learning outcomes.

Chart B. Central Broadcast Decision

Figure 4 presents Chart B. This chart is designed to identify the appropriate media to employ if a decision for centrally broadcasting the instruction has already been made. Chart B is presented early in the media selection process because a prior decision to broadcast instruction obviously limits the media options available.

Question 2. Central Broadcast? The choice of a broadcast system would most likely be an administrative decision made prior to the designer's involvement in the media selection process. Such a decision would appear to be appropriate if all of the following conditions are met:
  (a) students are dispersed over a wide geographic area;
  (b) transmission of the instructional message must be made from a central point, to be received by students at scheduled times; and
  (c) the message is transitory, that is, it does not require a preserved record after transmission.

If these conditions prevail, either broadcast TV or radio should be selected, and the designer should proceed to question 3. Otherwise, the flowchart leads the designer to question 7, which is contained in Chart C.

Question 3. Either an Attitude or Verbal Information? Is the instruction designed either to influence the student's values or opinions, or impart verbal information for recall? This double-barreled question is designed to divide the entire domain of learning

How to Use the Model

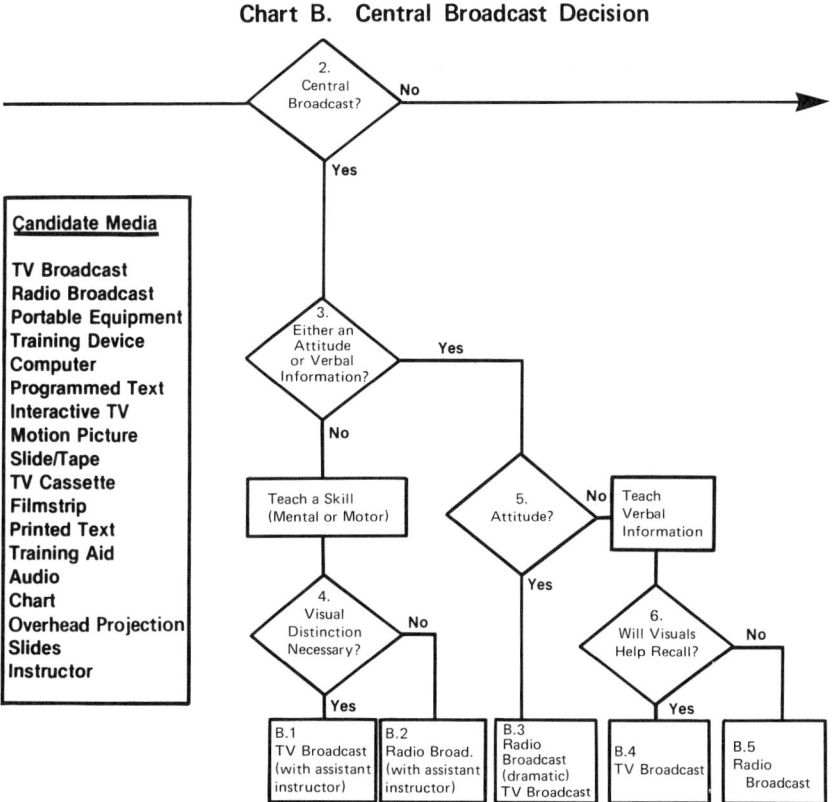

Explanation of Questions - Chart B

2. Central Broadcast? Is the instructional system designed to serve students who are dispersed over a wide geographic area and who are able to receive centrally broadcast instruction at scheduled times?
3. Either an Attitude or Verbal Information? Is the aim either to influence the student's values (attitudes) or to have the student learn to 'state' (rather than 'do') something?
4. Visual Distinction Necessary? Is the visual presentation of task features necessary or will it aid in learning the task?
5. Attitude? Does instruction aim to influence the student's values or opinions?
6. Will Visuals Help Recall? Is it likely that the use of visuals will help the student establish images that will aid recall of verbal information?

Figure 4. Flowchart panel pertaining to the "central broadcast decision."

outcomes into two major parts, the other part being skills, intellectual or motor. The meaning of attitude, a learned disposition that reflects the individual's value of choices, is fairly easy to comprehend. The second possibility is that the aim of instruction is to communicate some verbal information which can be recalled and "told about." For example, verbal information may be learned which enables the student to tell about the judicial functions of the Supreme Court. It may be noted that such recall is "declarative knowledge," not "procedural knowledge" (which is called here intellectual skill). Thus, a "yes" decision at this point means that what is to be learned is *either* an attitude or some items of verbal information. A "yes" answer to this question leads to a further decision which will separate the two.

A "no" answer to question 3 leads to the choice of skill as intellectual or motor. An intellectual skill enables the individual to apply a principle or rule to a particular instance (Gagné, 1977). An intellectual skill is involved, for example, when the sum of two numbers is calculated. A motor skill is required, for example, in executing a dance step or in using a hand tool.

Although they are to be distinguished in a later decision, intellectual and motor skills are related in their requirement for *precise feedback during learning*. If broadcast media are used, then the auditory or visual displays provided by the broadcast medium must be supplemented by a means for providing corrective feedback to student responses. Under these conditions, supplementary response booklets would normally be specified for the recording of student responses. As for the feedback itself, the requirement for an instructor comes to mind. However, if broadcast programs and the supplementary booklets are carefully designed, the limited function of providing corrective feedback may be performed by an assistant to the instructor.

Question 4. Visual Distinction Necessary? Can displayed pictures or diagrams aid in the distinguishing of task features? The task being learned may require differential responding to visual features. Map reading, for example, requires this kind of intellectual skill. If visual features must be distinguished, the question should be answered "yes." If the question is answered "yes," television broadcast (rather than radio) is selected. In accordance with the previous decision (question 3), the medium requires an assistant instructor to provide corrective feedback.

Question 5. Attitude? Does instruction aim to influence the student's values or opinions? An attitude is involved if instruction aims to influence the student's behavior in an area where he or she has some freedom to choose his or her own actions. Attitude instruction sometimes requires a background of skills and verbal information, but is itself aimed at quite a different learning outcome (Gagné, 1977).

If an attitude is the goal, probably the most effective media are those that are able to display "human models." These are respected persons who can indicate their satisfaction with the attitudinal choice (Bandura, 1969). So far as is known, this kind of display is the most effective for establishing or changing attitudes. Media such as slide/tape that can present only static images are likely to be somewhat less effective. Audio presentations are also somewhat less powerful in establishing attitudes. However, the use of techniques such as dramatic radio shows (involving fictional human models) must be acknowledged as having some effectiveness.

If the answer to the attitude question is "no," this means that the objective falls in the category of verbal information (something that is to be stated). An example is the verbal information a student in an American History course might have about the process of election of a United States President. The important feature of verbal information is that it is tested by oral or written recall. It involves the statement of facts or pieces of connected prose, but not the application of those facts.

Question 6. Will Visuals Help Recall? Is it likely that the use of visuals will help the student establish mental images that will aid the recall of verbal information? For example, as an item of information, a physics student might be required to describe the pattern of airflow around aircraft wings. If it appears that acquisition and retention of this knowledge can be enhanced by visual processing (using visual images), then the question should be answered "yes."

Precise estimation of the amount of advantage for visuals in teaching verbal information is not possible at the present time. The advantage exists, but must be weighed against other considerations. Factors favoring a choice of visual presentation are suggested by the following questions:

    (a) Is the information lengthy or complex?
    (b) Must the information be retained completely and accurately?
    (c) Must the information be retained over long periods of time?

If any of these conditions exist, the instructional designer will be aiming to select a learning strategy that provides effective cues for the retrieval of information that is learned. A visual medium selected by a "yes" answer at this point contributes to that aim.

Chart C. Self-Instruction with Readers

Chart C is shown in Figure 5. This chart is designed to identify the appropriate media for situations in which students who are proficient readers are expected to learn by self-instruction. The chart contains six questions, three of which are also included in Chart B, and have been described in the previous section. The three new questions are discussed in the following paragraphs.

Question 7. Self-Instruction? Are students expected to learn by self-instruction, without an instructor? (An instructor may, of course, manage a self-instructional operation for a group of students whom he or she does not actually teach.) When self-instructional procedures are employed, students are usually allowed to proceed through the instruction at their own pace.

How to Use the Model

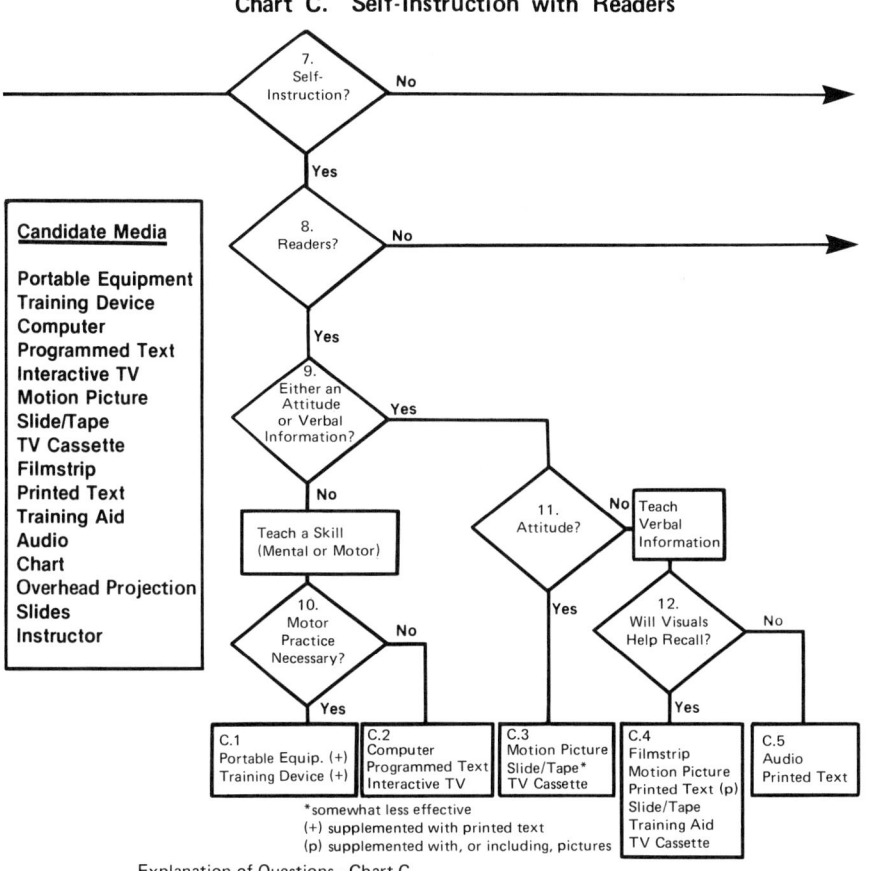

Figure 5. Flowchart panel applicable to the instructional situation "self-instruction with readers."

Self-pacing is especially important when there is a need for each individual to achieve mastery of tasks during training.

Question 8. Readers? Are the students capable of efficiently gaining information from printed materials? Varying degrees of reading ability may be expected among students. This question pertains to whether students are capable of following the meaning of a printed paragraph of instructional materials within a reasonably brief period of time. If students are capable of doing so, print media should be considered; otherwise only non-print media are appropriate.

Question 10. Motor Practice Necessary? Skills that involve the learning of smoothly timed muscular responses are called motor (or "psychomotor") skills. Motor skills can be learned to suitable degrees of refinement when the student directly practices the movements involved. Practice of this sort requires either the real object, such as a typewriter or a tennis racket, or a training device which "feels like" the real object. A "yes" answer to this question will lead the designer to choose between these two types of media. A "no" answer indicates that an intellectual skill is being taught, in which case a different set of media is to be considered.

It may be noted that a real object may have already been selected as a result of the designer's answer to question 1. In such cases, a "yes" answer here reaffirms the earlier selection. There may, however, be instances where the consequences of task error are not serious (the answer to question 1 is "no"), but motor practice is still necessary in order to acquire the skill. In these situations, a real object may still be an appropriate media choice.

Chart D. Self-Instruction with Non-Readers

Figure 6 presents Chart D. This chart is designed to identify the appropriate media when poor readers are expected to learn by self-instruction. The chart contains six questions, four of which appear in previous charts. The two new questions are discussed in the following paragraphs.

How to Use the Model 79

Chart D. Self-Instruction with Non-Readers

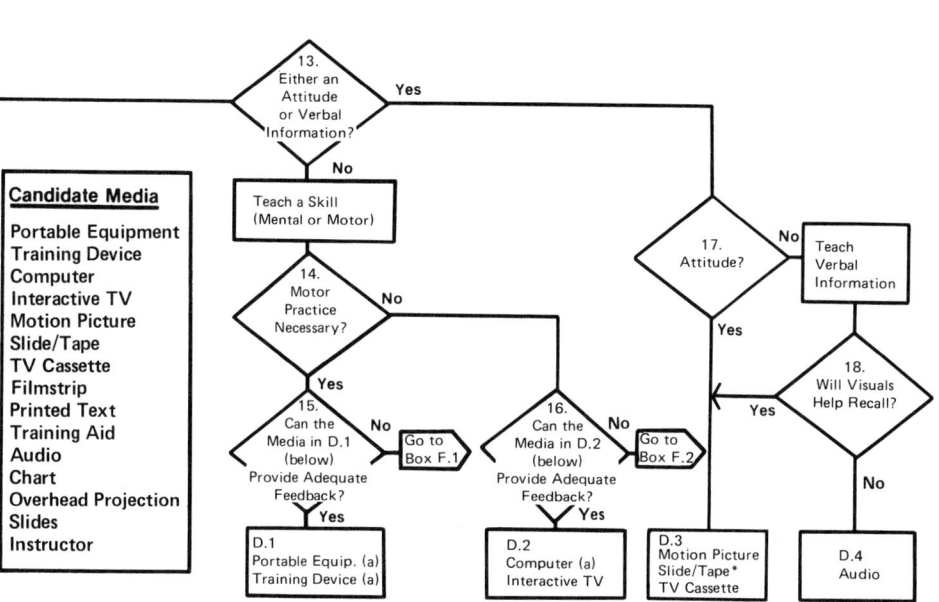

Explanation of Questions - Chart D

13. Either an Attitude or Verbal Information? Is the aim either to influence the student's values (attitudes) or to have the student learn to 'state' (rather than 'do') something?
14. Motor Practice Necessary? Does the skill to be learned require smooth timing of muscular movements (a "motor skill")?
15. Can the Media in D.1 Provide Adequate Feedback? Can the media in D.1 accept and evaluate the desired student responses and provide the type of feedback required?
16. Can the Media in D.2 Provide Adequate Feedback? Can the media in D.2 accept and evaluate the desired student responses and provide the type of feedback required?
17. Attitude? Does instruction aim to influence the student's values or opinions?
18. Will Visuals Help Recall? Is it likely that the use of visuals will help the student establish images that will aid recall of verbal information?

6.

Figure 6. Flowchart panel applicable to the instructional situation "self-instruction with non-readers."

Question 15. Can the Media in D.1 Provide Adequate Feedback? Will the media listed in "bottom-line" box D.1 accept and evaluate the required student responses and provide the type of feedback required by the learning outcomes? This question provides an opportunity to re-check the proposed training situation. For example, if a motor skill is being learned by poor readers, the possibility that this can be accomplished by self-instruction should now be re-evaluated, with the alternative choice of instructor-led training a possibility.

An example of the usefulness of the "re-check" question is as follows. A learning activity may require students to solder a wire to a connector within a piece of electronic equipment. Neither portable equipment nor a training device (the media listed in box D.1) can provide adequate feedback on this task, since feedback requires a visual inspection of the soldered joint. An instructor or an assistant instructor will likely be necessary, in which case the choice of media shifts to those in box F.1.

Question 16. Can the Media in D.2 Provide Adequate Feedback? Will the media listed in "bottom-line" box D.2 accept and evaluate the required student responses and provide the type of feedback indicated in the learning activities? This, too, is a question providing for a re-check of the training situation. If a mental skill is being learned by poor readers, the possibility that this can be accomplished by self-instruction should now be re-evaluated, with the choice of instructor-led training an alternate possibility.

For example, a learning activity may require students to write a clearly written business letter. Neither a computer nor interactive television (the media listed in D.2) can evaluate a written response for clarity. An instructor or assistant instructor will doubtless be necessary, and the choice of media shifts to those in box F.2.

Chart E. Instructor with Readers

Figure 7 displays Chart E. This chart identifies the appropriate

How to Use the Model

Chart E. Instructor with Readers

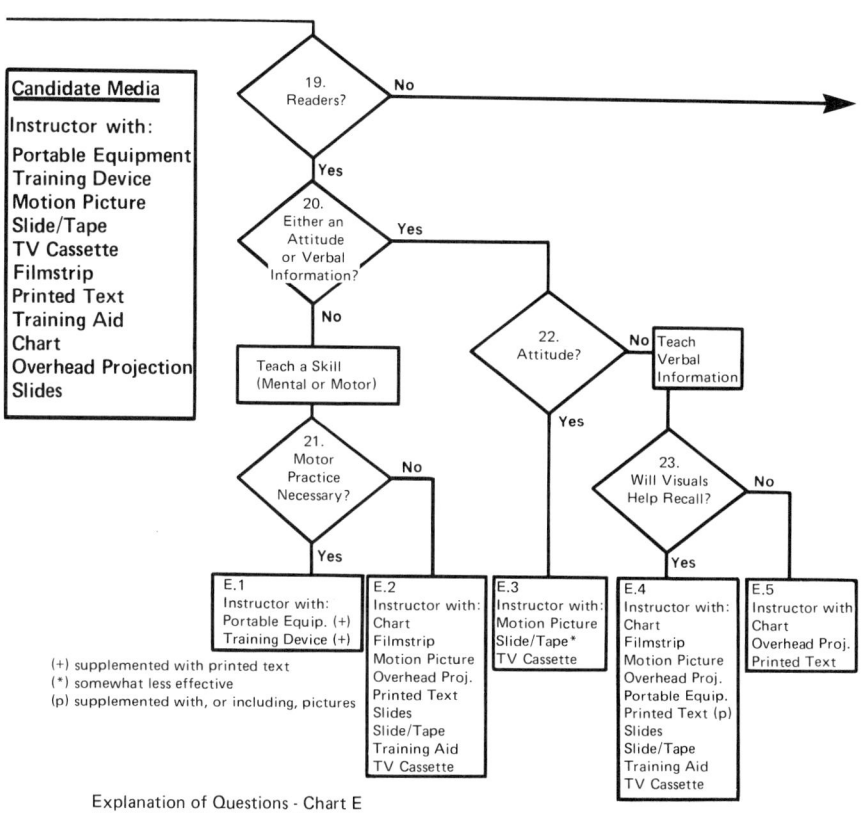

Explanation of Questions - Chart E

19. Readers? Can the students, with reasonable efficiency, gain information from printed text?
20. Either an Attitude or Verbal Information? Is the aim either to influence the student's values (attitudes) or to have the student learn to 'state' (rather than 'do') something?
21. Motor Practice Necessary? Does the skill to be learned require smooth timing of muscular movements (a "motor skill")?
22. Attitude? Does instruction aim to influence the student's values or opinions?
23. Will Visuals Help Recall? Is it likely that the use of visuals will help the student establish images that will aid recall of verbal information?

Figure 7. Flowchart panel applicable to the instructional situation "instructor with readers."

media for students who are proficient readers and who are to be taught by an instructor. The chart contains five questions, each of which appears in a previous chart.

Chart F. Instructor with Non-Readers

Figure 8 presents Chart F. This chart identifies the appropriate media for students who are poor readers and are to be taught by an instructor. The chart contains four questions, each of which has been previously described.

Final Selection Procedure

When a box on the bottom line of the flowchart is reached, the designer places a check mark by each of the listed media in the Media Selection Worksheet. After the flowchart has been used to identify the appropriate media for each objective or set of objectives in the lesson or module from among those media checked on the worksheet, a final selection decision may now be made. Either a single medium or a combination of media may be selected from among those media checked on the worksheet. Arriving at a final choice makes use of the following procedure:

1. *Eliminate media* by crossing off those which are not feasible in the situation for which instruction is being designed. The following questions are relevant:
    (a) Can the medium be produced by the time needed?
    (b) Can the costs of production, maintenance, and operation be afforded?
    (c) Can the medium be approved as compatible with existing policies and programs?
    (d) Is the medium practical for use in its intended environment?

2. *Make a final choice of media.* Consider the following questions:

How to Use the Model

Chart F. Instructor with Non-Readers

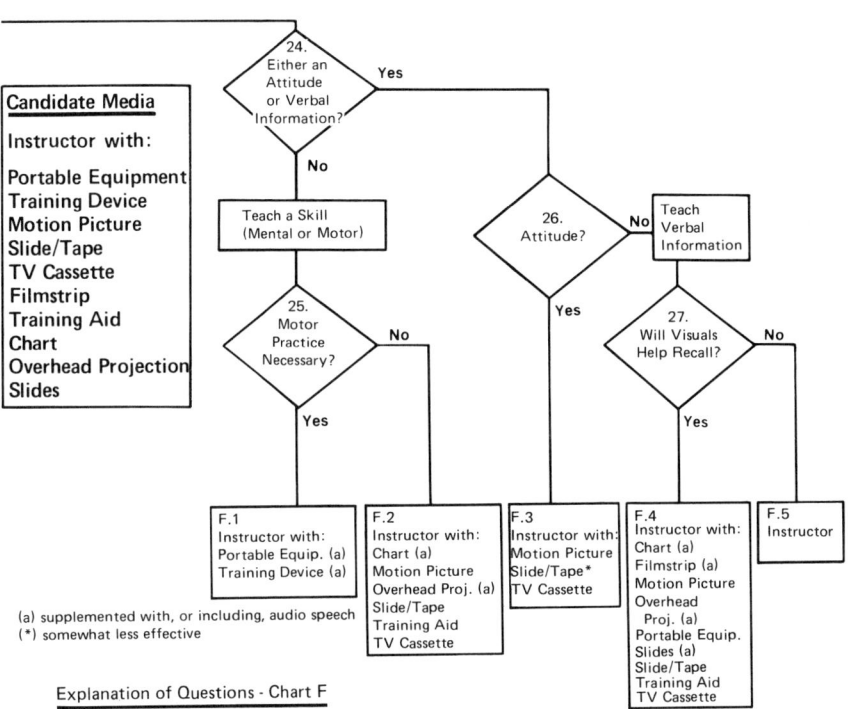

Explanation of Questions - Chart F

24. Either an Attitude or Verbal Information? Is the aim either to influence the student's values (attitudes) or to have the student learn to 'state' (rather than 'do') something?
25. Motor Practice Necessary? Does the skill to be learned require smooth timing of muscular movements (a "motor skill")?
26. Attitude? Does instruction aim to influence the student's values or opinions?
27. Will Visuals Help Recall? Is it likely that the use of visuals will help the student establish images that will aid recall of verbal information?

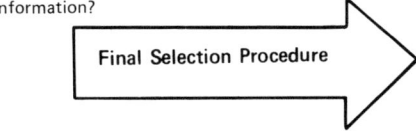

8.

Figure 8. Flowchart panel applicable to the instructional situation "instructor with non-readers."

(a) Is more than one medium necessary to enable students to learn all of the objectives?
(b) What are the comparative costs of the final candidate media and media combinations?
(c) Can each medium meet the estimated requirements for change and updating?

The final selection procedure, as described here, allows the designer to consider practical factors such as cost and production time, but only after full consideration has been given to factors favorable to learning. Both sets of factors, those relating to learning effectiveness and those affecting practical usage, are important in the media selection process. It will be apparent that we favor a procedure which gives temporal priority to the assessment of media characteristics affecting learning.

References

Bandura, A. *Principles of behavior modification.* New York: Holt, Rinehart, and Winston, 1969.

Gagné, R.M. *The conditions of learning* (3rd ed.). New York: Holt, Rinehart, and Winston, 1977.

Chapter 6

Examples of the Model in Use

This chapter contains five examples that illustrate how the model works. Each involves a different learning situation, that is, a different instructional setting, a different domain of learning outcome, and different expectations about the reading ability of intended learners. These learning situations are summarized in Table 2; see the following page.

Example 1—Broadcast Instruction, Adult Education

The education director for a consortium of retirement communities in a large metropolitan area has been asked to design an instructional program intended to get the residents of these communities to become more active in local politics. The director has determined that in order for the program to reach a large percentage of these people, it should be presented on either the local educational television station or the local educational radio station. Both stations have time slots devoted to programs for senior citizens, and a market survey has indicated that a large percentage of retirees tune in to the programs broadcast during these hours.

The director does not have a budget that can support the development of both a radio and a television program, and so must choose one of these media. She uses the media selection flowchart to help arrive at a media choice.

Table 2

Summary Descriptions of the Learning Situations Represented by the Five Examples in This Chapter

Example Number	Instructional Setting	Objective(s)	Domain of Learning	Learner Reading Ability
1	Broadcast Instruction, Adult Education	Participate in the political process	Attitude	Some good, some poor
2	Self-Instruction, Science Education	(a) State names of units of metric linear measure	Verbal Information	Good
	Self-Instruction, Science Education	(b) Perform metric conversion	Intellectual Skill	Good
3	Classroom Instruction, Vocational Education	Identify causes of a malfunctioning air conditioner	Intellectual Skill	Poor
4	Classroom Instruction, Sales Training	Calculate financing charges	Intellectual Skill	Good
5	Self-Instruction, Military Training	Assemble a radio antenna	Motor Skill	Poor

Examples of the Model in Use

The first page of the flowchart lists the type of information that should be gathered prior to using the chart. The director collects this information, which consists of the following:
- (1) the objective to be taught: viewers of the program will choose to participate in the local political process;
- (2) the domain of learning outcome to which the objective belongs: attitude;
- (3) the setting in which the instruction will take place: central broadcast; and
- (4) whether or not the learners are expected to be competent readers: many will be competent readers, many will not.

Having collected this information, the director begins to make use of the flowchart. When the chart is entered at the point labeled "Start Here," the first step is to use the Media Selection Worksheet to record the objective. An abbreviated version of the objective is written at the top of the first column of the worksheet.

Coming now to the flowchart, the first question asks whether the consequences of task error are serious. This question is usually not applicable when an attitude is the objective. Since an attitude is involved in this case, the answer "no" is made to question 1.

Question 2 asks whether the instruction will be presented via central broadcast media. Having decided that either radio or television will be used to deliver the program, the director answers the question in the affirmative and proceeds to question 3, which asks whether the objective being worked with is an attitude or verbal information. A "yes" answer signifies that the objective involves either an attitude or verbal information. A "no" answer indicates that *neither* an attitude nor verbal information is involved. Since the objective of the planned program is an attitude, a "yes" answer is given to this question.

A "yes" answer to question 3 leads to question 5, which confirms the objective as an attitude objective, leading to another "yes" answer.

The director now proceeds to box B.3, located along the bottom line of the flowchart. This box lists the candidate media appropriate for the given instructional situation. In this case, either a dramatic radio broadcast or a TV broadcast is shown as being appropriate for encouraging senior citizens to participate in the local political process. The director places check marks next to these options in the first column of the Media Selection Worksheet. She also records that the radio broadcast should be dramatic in composition.

If the program for which media were being chosen had other objectives associated with it, the director would now identify the candidate media for those other objectives before making any final selection decision. In this instance, however, no other objectives have been included, so a final selection decision can be made at this point.

The last page of the flowchart lists some questions to be considered when a final selection decision is to be made. Upon reviewing these questions, the director concludes that producing the TV broadcast would be much more costly than producing the radio show. Given this conclusion, and the fact that both media have been identified as appropriate, the director chooses to use a radio broadcast. A radio show will be designed to encourage senior citizens to participate in local political activities.

Example 2—Self-Instruction, Science Education

In an affluent suburban school district, administrators have decided that the junior high school's individualized science program should include a unit on the metric system. The science education supervisor for the district has been asked to supervise the development of the self-instructional modules that will constitute the unit.

The supervisor is currently planning a module on linear

Examples of the Model in Use 89

measurement and must decide upon the instructional media that will be used. He employs the media selection flowchart to help him make this decision.

The first step the supervisor takes is to gather the information he needs in order to use the flowchart. That information is as follows:

(1) the objectives to be taught:
   a. the learner will state that the units of measure that are 1/1000th, 1/100th, and 1/10th of a meter are called, respectively, a millimeter, a centimeter, and a decimeter; and
   b. given a measure of length expressed in either inches, feet, or yards, the learner will calculate the equivalent metric measure in millimeters, centimeters, decimeters, and meters;
(2) the domains of learning outcomes to which the objectives belong: the first objective involves verbal information, the second objective involves an intellectual skill;
(3) the setting in which the instruction will take place: the module will be used in a self-instructional setting; and
(4) whether or not the learners are expected to be competent readers: the students who participate in the individualized science program are skillful readers.

This lesson involves two objectives that fall into different domains; therefore, it is necessary to proceed through the flowchart with each objective separately. Since a final media selection decision should be deferred until all candidate media for both objectives have been identified, it does not matter which objective is examined first. In this case, the science education supervisor decides to use the flowchart initially to identify the candidate media for objective (a). He lists this objective in the first column of the Media Selection Worksheet that accompanies the flowchart.

Having identified the objective, the supervisor proceeds to the first flowchart question, which asks, "When the student is first required to perform the task outside of the instructional setting, are the consequences of error serious?" Being unable to correctly name the units of measure that are 1/10th, 1/100th, and 1/1000th of a meter is not likely to cause serious consequences; the answer to this question is "no."

A "no" answer to question 1 leads directly to question 2, whether the instruction will be delivered via central broadcast media. In this case, a prior decision to use central broadcast media has not been made, nor is there any indication that the instructional situation fits the conditions under which central broadcast media are most appropriate. That is, there is no indication that the lesson is being designed to serve students who are widely dispersed *and* who can receive centrally broadcast instruction at scheduled times. Therefore, the answer to question 2 is "no."

With a "no" answer to question 2, the flowchart leads to question 7, which asks if the learners are expected to learn by self-instruction. In this case, the answer to the question is "yes," so the procedure now leads to question 8, which asks whether the learners are competent readers. The answer to this question is also "yes."

The next question is number 9, concerning the matter of whether the objective being worked with is either an attitude or verbal information. This means that if the objective involved either an attitude or verbal information, the answer to this question would be "yes." Since in this case the objective comprises verbal information, the question is answered in the affirmative. The diagram now leads to question 11, which should be answered "no," since an attitude is not being taught. At this point, the supervisor encounters a rectangular box confirming that verbal information is to be the outcome of the instruction.

Question 12 is now encountered, asking whether visuals will help the learner recall the verbal information to be learned.

Examples of the Model in Use   *91*

Although a case could be made for either answer to this question, it seems likely that visuals will help learners recall the names of metric measures, so the answer is "yes." This answer leads to box C.4, which lists the candidate media that are appropriate for this kind of objective under the instructional circumstances previously outlined. The media in this box may now be check-marked in the first column of the Media Selection Worksheet. A sample of a marked worksheet is shown in Figure 9.

Now that the appropriate candidate media for objective (a) have been identified, the same thing must be done for objective (b). After listing that objective in the second column of the Media Selection Worksheet, the supervisor proceeds to question 1 of the flowchart. This question is answered "no." Miscalculating the metric equivalents of U.S. linear measures may be serious in some special situations, but not in most cases.

The next four questions arrived at (questions 2, 7, 8, and 9) are the same ones encountered when the appropriate media for objective (a) were being identified. Answers to the first three of these questions are the same as before ("no" to 2, "yes" to 7, "yes" to 8). Question 9, however, receives a different answer.

Objective (b) is neither an attitude nor verbal information; it is an intellectual skill. Accordingly, the answer to question 9 is "no." This answer leads to a rectangular box indicating that either an intellectual (mental) or motor skill is to be taught.

The supervisor now proceeds to question 10, which asks whether motor practice of the skill is necessary. If the skill were a motor skill, the answer to this question would be "yes." The intellectual skill of converting U.S. linear measures to their equivalent metric measures, however, is not a motor skill, so the answer to question 10 is "no."

Box C.2 is now arrived at. This box lists the appropriate candidate media for objective (b) within the instructional situation specified. These media may be check-marked in the appropriate column of the Media Selection Worksheet. A sample of an appropriately marked worksheet is shown in Figure 10.

MEDIA SELECTION WORKSHEET

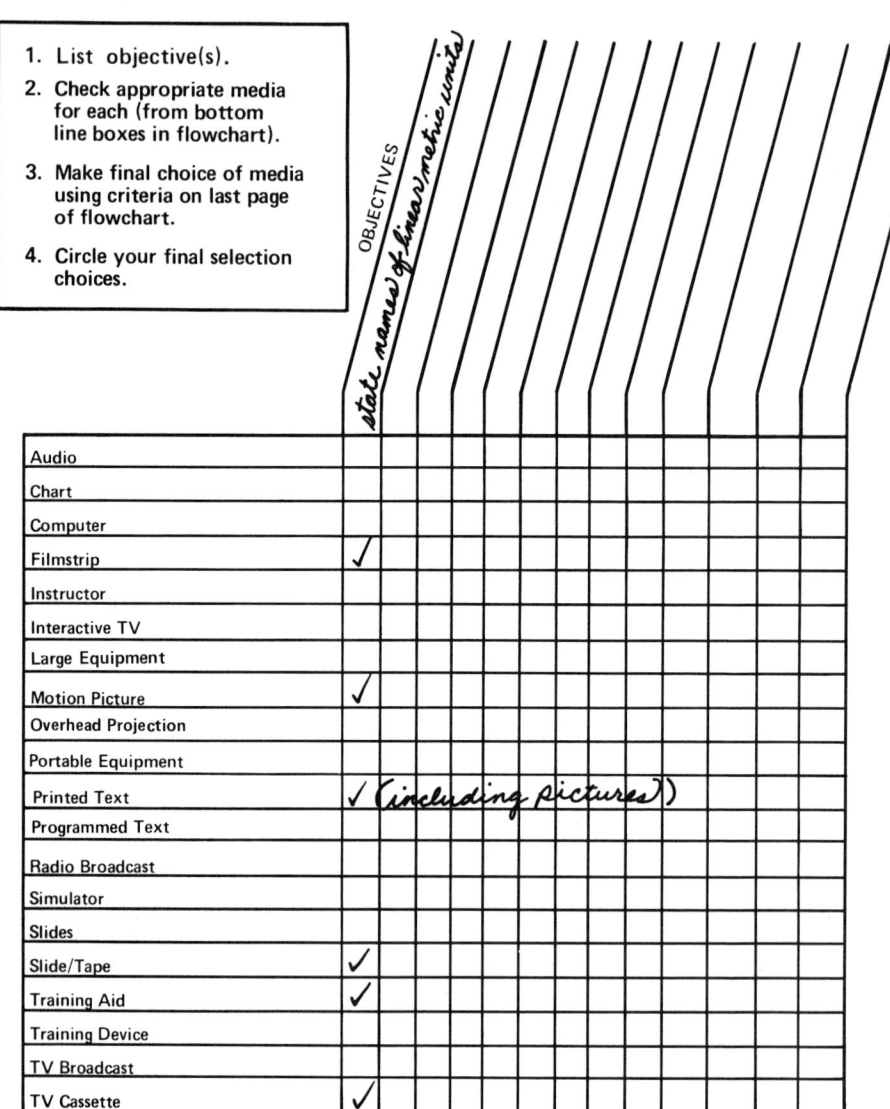

Figure 9. Entries in the Media Selection Worksheet for the objective "state names of linear metric units."

Examples of the Model in Use

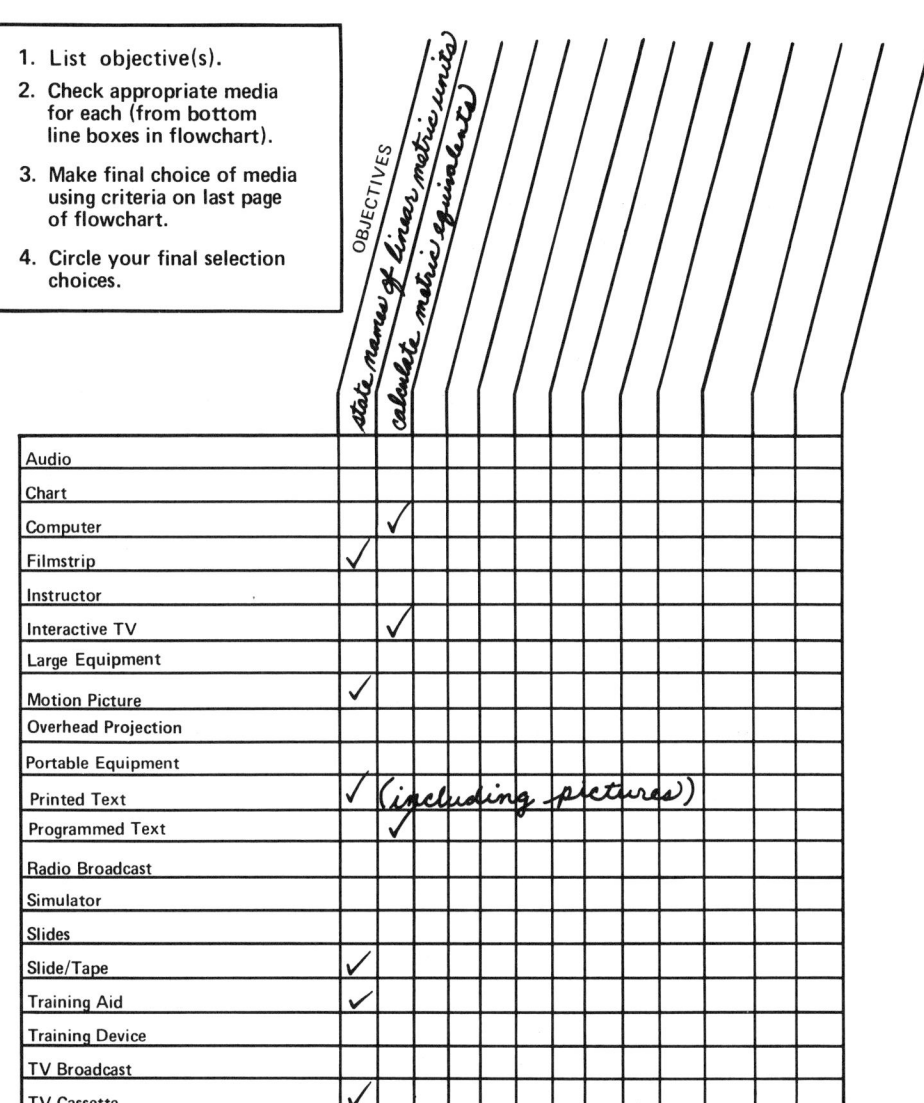

Figure 10. Entries in the Media Selection Worksheet for the objectives "state names of linear metric units" and "calculate metric equivalents."

The supervisor has now identified the appropriate candidate media for the two objectives of the module, and must now make a final media selection decision. Referring to the first group of questions on the last page of the flowchart, he decides that, on the basis of cost, interactive TV and the computer should be eliminated as candidate media. He also decides that the time necessary to produce a film or TV cassette is too great, and takes note that the hardware available in the junior high school does not permit the use of slide/tape.

Five of the nine candidate media have now been eliminated, and the supervisor must choose from among the remaining four (filmstrip, programmed text, printed text with pictures, and a training aid). A programmed text, being the only candidate medium left for objective (b), is selected. As for the other media, reference is now made to the second group of questions on the last page of the flowchart. After reviewing these questions, the decision is made that print materials supplemented with pictures should also be used. The cost of producing the programmed text along with the other print materials would be relatively low, and since all the materials would be in print form, they would be easy to revise. Therefore, the supervisor's final media choice is to develop print materials, a portion of which will be supplemented by pictures, and a portion of which will be in the form of programmed instruction.

Example 3—Classroom Instruction, Vocational Education

An instructor in a vocational school has been asked to develop a new course to train students to repair air conditioners. The instructor decides that one of the primary goals of the course should be to have students learn the probable causes of various types of malfunctions. He begins to develop a lesson on this topic, using the media selection flowchart to help him choose the media that might be employed during the lesson.

Examples of the Model in Use

Prior to using the flowchart, the instructor gathers some relevant information, as follows:

(1) the objective to be taught: given a malfunctioning air conditioner, the learner will identify the probable causes of the problem;

(2) the domain of learning outcome to which the objective belongs: intellectual skills;

(3) the setting in which the instruction will take place: classroom setting, with the instructor serving as the primary source of instruction;

(4) whether or not the learners are expected to be competent readers: most of the students in the class will not be competent readers.

The instructor lists the objective at the top of the first column of the Media Selection Worksheet and begins to follow the flowchart. The first question encountered is whether the consequences of task error are serious. The instructor decides that serious consequences may result from a failure to identify correctly the probable cause of an air conditioning malfunction. The answer to question 1, therefore, is "yes."

The flowchart now leads to box A.1, which indicates that large (real) equipment, portable (real) equipment, and a simulator are appropriate media candidates under these conditions. Check marks are placed next to these media in the first column of the Media Selection Worksheet (see Figure 11).

In order to identify other media appropriate for the course, flowchart question 2 is addressed next. Since a live instructor is to serve as the primary source of instruction in this instance, the answer to question 2 ("Central Broadcast?") is "no." For the same reason, the answer to the next question, question 7 ("Self-Instruction?"), is also "no."

A "no" answer to question 7 takes the instructor to question 19, which asks whether the learners are competent readers. Most of the learners in this instance are known not to be competent

MEDIA SELECTION WORKSHEET

1. List objective(s).
2. Check appropriate media for each (from bottom line boxes in flowchart).
3. Make final choice of media using criteria on last page of flowchart.
4. Circle your final selection choices.

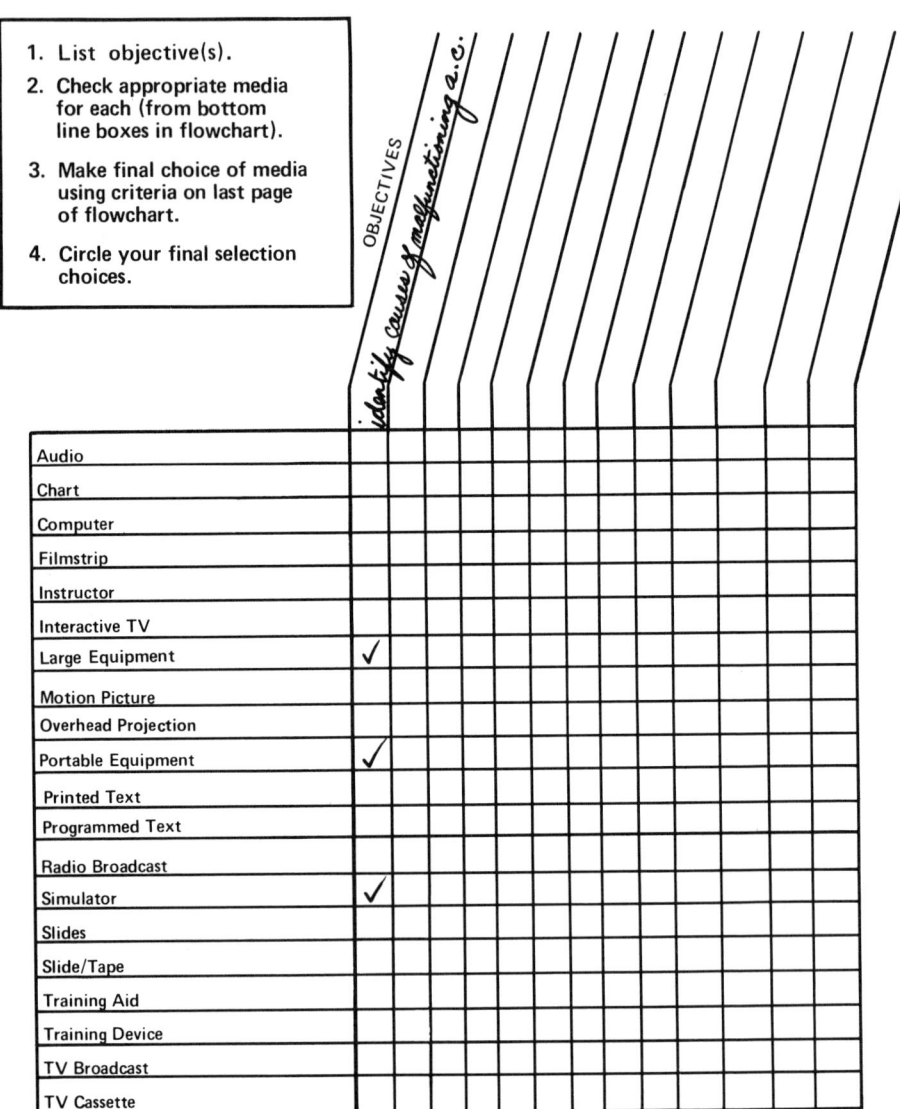

	identify causes of malfunctioning a.c.
Audio	
Chart	
Computer	
Filmstrip	
Instructor	
Interactive TV	
Large Equipment	✓
Motion Picture	
Overhead Projection	
Portable Equipment	✓
Printed Text	
Programmed Text	
Radio Broadcast	
Simulator	✓
Slides	
Slide/Tape	
Training Aid	
Training Device	
TV Broadcast	
TV Cassette	

Figure 11. Initial entries in the Media Selection Worksheet for the objective "identify causes of a malfunctioning air conditioner."

Examples of the Model in Use 97

readers; the answer to question 19 is "no." This response leads in turn to question 24.

Question 24, like some of the earlier questions in the flowchart, asks whether the targeted objective is an attitude or verbal information. Since the objective in this example involves neither an attitude nor verbal information, but rather an intellectual skill, the answer to question 24 is "no." The flowchart now exhibits a rectangular box confirming that a skill is to be taught. Question 25 asks whether motor practice of the skill is necessary. The answer to this question is "no," a decision which leads to box F.2.

The media in box F.2 are the appropriate options for the intended instruction. Check marks are placed next to these media in the first column of the Media Selection Worksheet. The worksheet now appears as shown in Figure 12.

The instructor must now choose from among the candidate media that have been identified. He reviews the first group of questions on the last page of the flowchart and, based upon his answers, eliminates several media from further consideration. A motion picture, a simulator, a slide/tape presentation, and a TV cassette are eliminated in view of their cost. Portable equipment is also eliminated because of a determination that most of the air conditioners the course graduates are likely to service will not be portable.

The instructor chooses large equipment and overhead projections as media for incorporation into the course. This decision is based on a consideration of the second group of questions on the last page of the flowchart, as well as on other factors. If the large equipment, namely an actual air conditioning unit, is rigged so as to malfunction for various reasons, it can be used for demonstration purposes and can also be used to enable the individual students to practice the skill being taught. In addition, overhead projections can be used to present visual drawings that will aid the learner in following the instructor's presentation. For example, a wiring diagram can be displayed via an overhead projection. While a

MEDIA SELECTION WORKSHEET

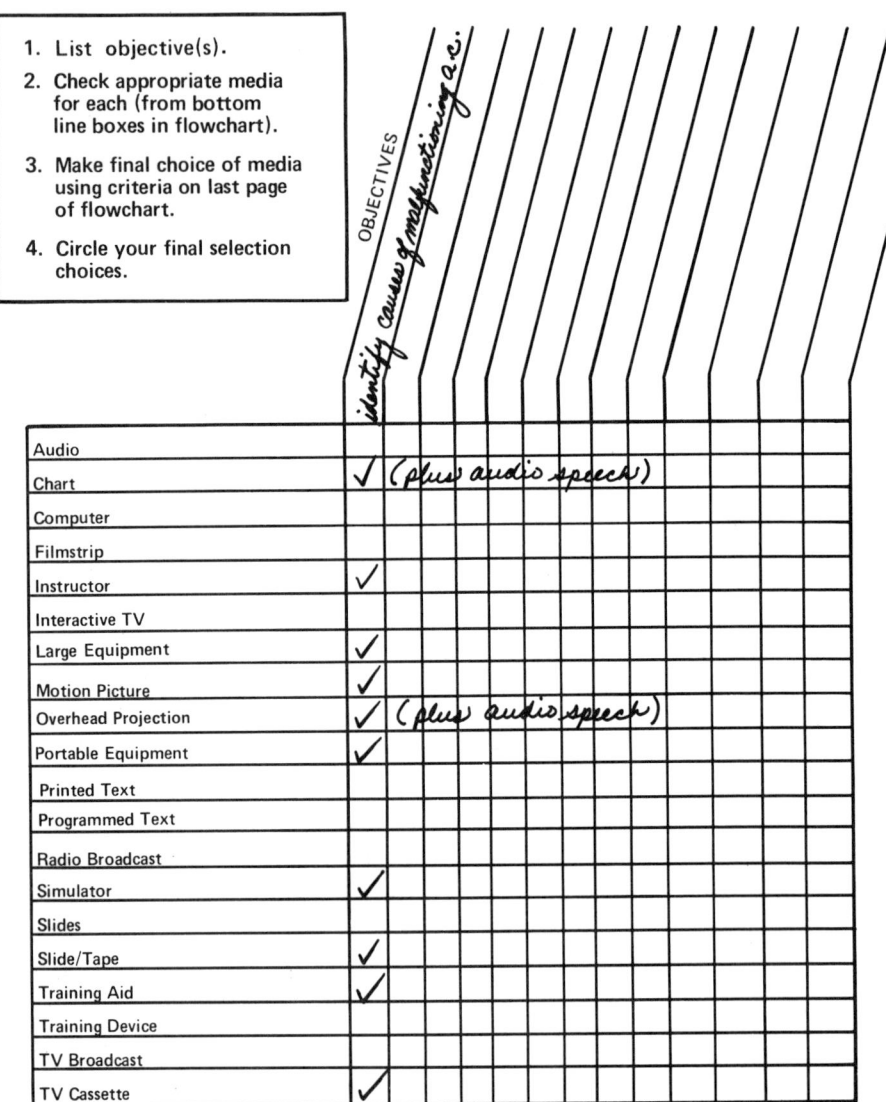

Figure 12. Complete set of entries in the Media Selection Worksheet for the objective "identify causes of a malfunctioning air conditioner."

Examples of the Model in Use   99

chart or training aid might also be used for this purpose, the cost of producing an overhead transparency is likely to be less. Furthermore, as new wiring schemes are incorporated into air conditioning units, displays of these schemes can be produced cheaply and quickly.

Example 4—Classroom Instruction, Sales Training

A large retail chain in a major metropolitan area is planning to introduce a new company-operated financing policy for their customers. Since sales personnel will be responsible for explaining the policy to customers, the company is planning a series of workshops designed to train the sales staff in the new policy.

One of the workshop goals is to enable the sales staff to calculate the total financing charge that will be paid by a customer who uses the policy. The training director for the company, who will be conducting the workshops, is planning a lesson designed to teach this skill.

Before using the media selection flowchart, the training director notes the following information:

(1) the objective to be taught: using a calculator, sales personnel will calculate the total financing charges a customer will pay if the customer uses the company-operated financing policy to purchase merchandise;

(2) the domain of learning outcome to which the objective belongs: intellectual skills;

(3) the setting in which the instruction will take place: classroom setting, with the training director serving as the primary source of instruction; and

(4) whether or not the trainees are expected to be competent readers: members of the sales staff can read well.

The training director lists the objective in the first column of the Media Selection Worksheet and proceeds to the first flowchart question, which asks whether the consequences of on-the-job task error are serious. The director decides that since the miscalculation of finance charges does not directly endanger people, the answer to question 1 is "no."

The director now proceeds to question 2 ("Central Broadcast?"). Since the workshop will be conducted live by the training director, the answer to this question is "no." The same answer also holds true for question 7 ("Self-Instruction?").

The next question encountered is question 19 ("Readers?"), which is answered "yes," since the sales staff can read well. Question 20 is now addressed, and it is answered "no," since the objective is neither an attitude nor verbal information. The flowchart now presents a rectangular box which confirms that a skill (in this case, an intellectual skill) is to be taught.

Question 21 is the last flowchart question addressed. It is answered in the negative, since motor practice is not necessary in order for sales personnel to perform the objective. A "no" answer to question 21 leads to box E.2, which lists the candidate media for the specified instructional situation. The director checks these media in the appropriate column of the Media Selection Worksheet. A sample of the worksheet, with the candidate media listed in box E.2 check-marked, is shown in Figure 13.

The training director now must choose which of the candidate media she will use. As she reviews the first group of questions on the last page of the flowchart, she eliminates, on the basis of cost, filmstrips, motion pictures, slides, slide/tapes, and TV cassettes as candidate media. She also decides that printed text is impractical for use in the workshop environment and that training aids are inappropriate for the training situation.

Choosing from among the remaining media, the director decides that she will use a chalkboard and an overhead projector to support her classroom instruction. She chooses these media because they can be used easily in combination and both are appropriate, yet inexpensive, means of presenting examples of the calculations sales personnel will be required to perform.

Examples of the Model in Use

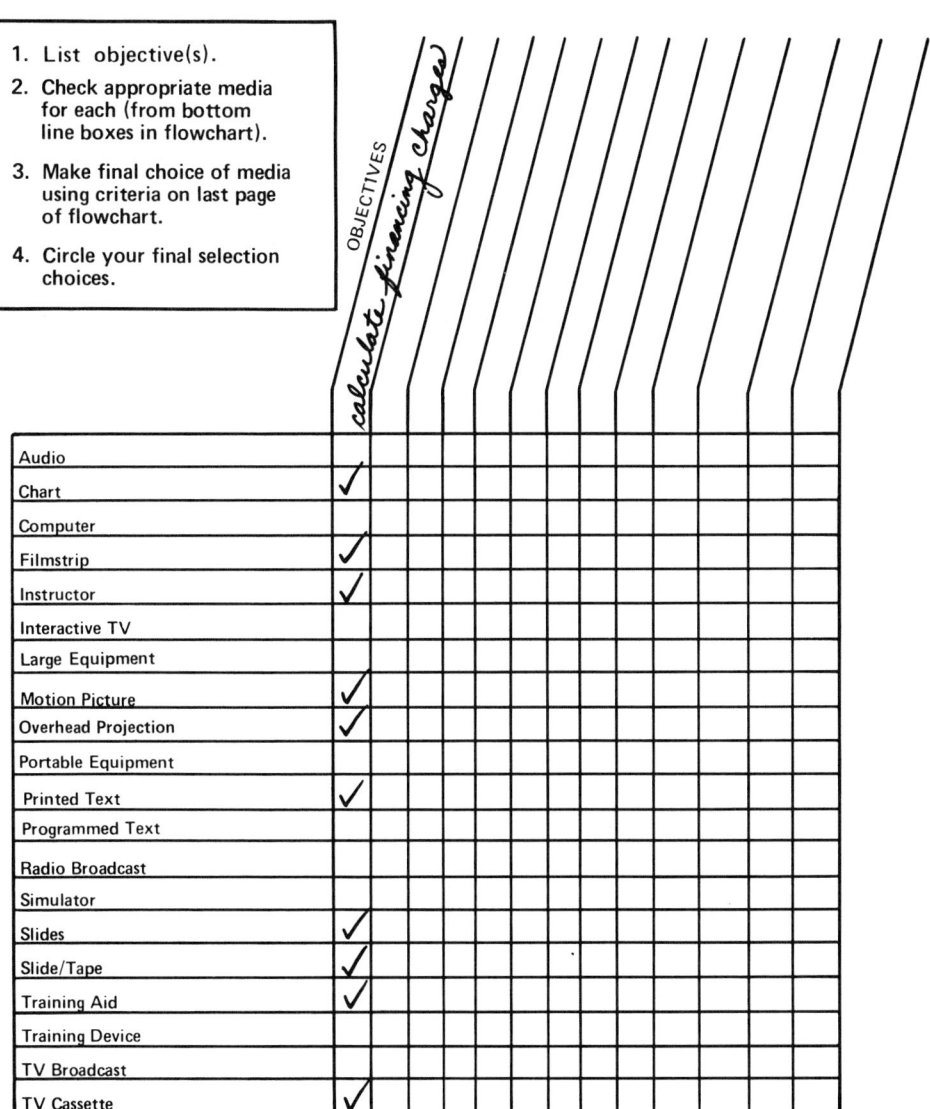

Figure 13. Entries in the Media Selection Worksheet for the objective "calculate financing charges."

Example 5—Self-Instruction, Military Training

The Army has purchased some new radio equipment that trainees must be taught how to operate and maintain. One of the tasks trainees must be taught is how to assemble the short antenna for the equipment. An education specialist employed by the Army has been assigned to design self-instructional materials that will enable trainees to perform this task.

In order to help him select the appropriate instructional media to employ, the education specialist uses the media selection flowchart. He begins by listing the following information:

(1) the objective to be taught: the soldier will properly assemble the short antenna for radio set XYZ (the new radio equipment);

(2) the domain of learning outcome to which the objective belongs: motor skills;

(3) the setting in which the instruction will take place: a learning center at an Army school (a self-instructional setting). The center is supervised by a non-commissioned officer (NCO) who provides instructional assistance to trainees when necessary; and

(4) whether or not the trainees are expected to be competent readers: most of the trainees will not be competent readers.

The objective is listed in the first column of the Media Selection Worksheet. The education specialist then begins to work through the flowchart. He responds to the first flowchart question ("Consequences of Task Error Serious?") in the negative, and so proceeds to question 2 ("Central Broadcast?") on the flowchart. Since the instruction being designed is expected to be self-instructional and is not intended to serve students dispersed over a wide geographic area, the answer to question 2 is "no." The answer to the next question, question 7 ("self-instruction?"), however, is "yes."

Question 8 ("Readers?") is now encountered and is answered "no," which leads the education specialist to question 13 ("Either an Attitude or Verbal Information?"). Since the objective being

Examples of the Model in Use

taught does not fall into either of these domains of learning, the answer to question 13 is "no," which leads to a box confirming that the objective being taught is a skill. Since the skill is a motor skill, the answer to the next question, question 14 ("Motor Practice Necessary?"), is "yes."

The education specialist now comes to question 15, which asks whether the media listed in box D.1 (portable equipment and a training device) can provide the trainees with adequate feedback as they assemble the short antenna. Since the errors trainees make may not be readily apparent to them as they work with a training device or portable equipment (i.e., the antenna itself), it is decided that neither medium can provide adequate feedback. Therefore, question 15 is answered "no," which leads the education specialist to box F.1 of the flowchart.

The candidate media listed in box F.1 are the candidate media from among which the education specialist will choose. These media are check-marked on the Media Selection Worksheet (see Figure 14).

The first set of questions on the last page of the flowchart are now referred to in order to help choose from among the candidate media. Based on the criterion of practicality, a training device is eliminated as a media choice. Thus, the remaining candidate media are portable equipment (supplemented with audio) and an instructor. The education specialist decides that each of these media, plus one other, will be used.

The final combination of media decided upon includes an audiotape, some drawings of the antenna parts, the antenna in its unassembled form, and an instructor. The audiotape and drawings will be used to describe how to assemble the antenna. The audiotape also will direct the trainees to attempt to assemble the antenna by following the directions given via the tape. Feedback regarding the adequacy of the trainees' performance will be provided by the NCO who supervises the learning center where the training will take place.

104   Selecting Media for Instruction

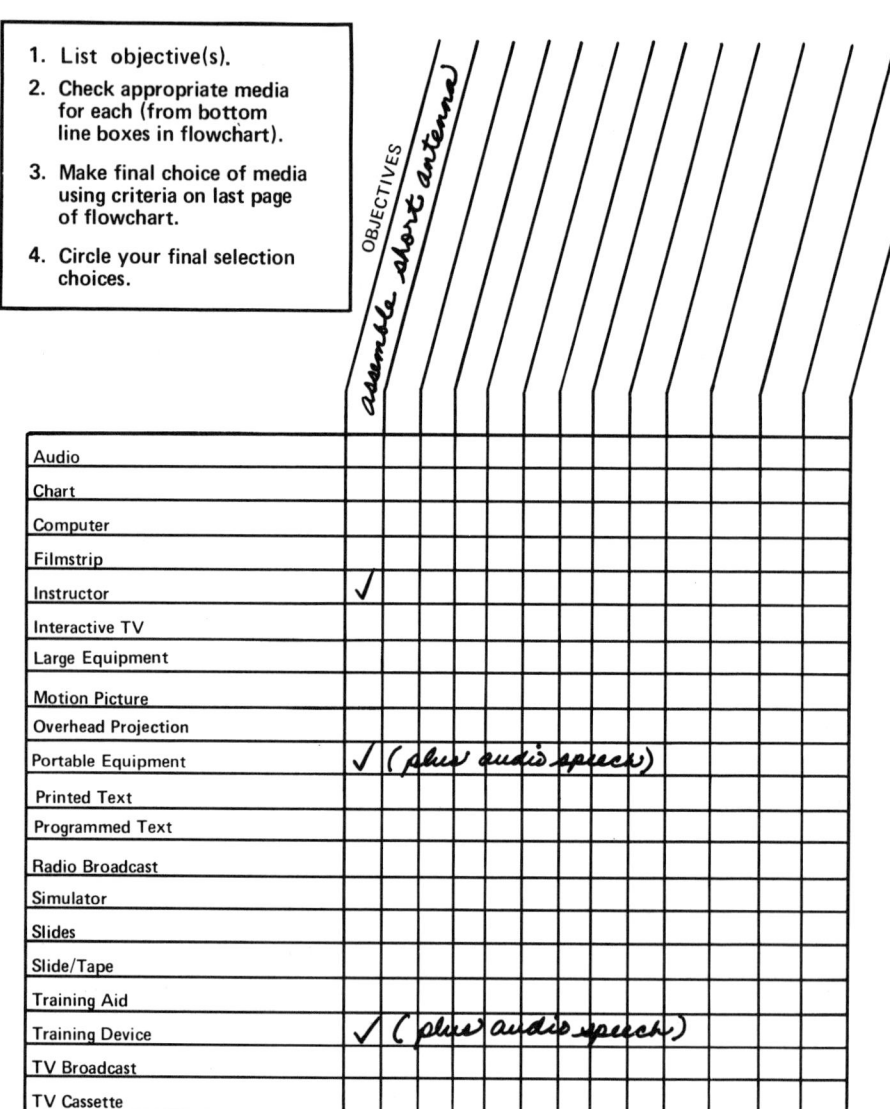

Figure 14. Entries in the Media Selection Worksheet for the objective "assemble short antenna."

Summary and Conclusion

The examples employed in this chapter indicate that the model can be used in a wide variety of situations. Appropriate media can be chosen for instruction which is broadcast, delivered by an instructor in a classroom, intended for learner self-instruction, or designed for acquiring practical skills with real equipment. The choice of media in any of these situations is influenced by the expected reading skills of the learners. And critical choices among media are determined by the kind of learning outcome aimed for: whether knowledge, skill, or attitude. Once these factors have been taken into account, the instructional designer can be confident that the remaining set of media will assure learning effectiveness. Final media decisions can then be based upon such practical factors as cost and availability.

Chapter 7

The Model's Potential

Of what value is the media selection model described in this book? What are its potential uses? How can its worth be judged? In this chapter, we will attempt to suggest some answers to these questions. Most of our answers will be based on best guesses as to what might come about. Some answers, however, will be based upon information we have already gathered, data we collected during the formative evaluation of the model. It is this evaluation that will be described first.

Evaluating the Model

The model presented in this book is a revised version of a model originally developed for the U.S. Army Research Institute, intended for use in the design of Army training. The Army model went through four cycles of review and revision (formative evaluation). Each cycle provided data that were useful in revising the model. The first formative evaluation cycle employed 21 instructional designers who were not directly involved in the initial development of the model. They were asked to review the model and offer suggestions as to how it might be improved. Each designer reviewed the model independently and either prepared a written list of suggested changes or provided an oral report which was recorded.

Following a review of comments from all of the designers,

numerous changes in the model were decided upon. Most frequently, the changes involved the wording used on the flowchart, and the definitions of media. After this initial evaluation cycle was completed, a formal procedure for evaluating the model was developed. This procedure was used during the second, third, and fourth formative evaluation cycles. Its purpose was to ascertain how successfully an instructional designer who had not seen the model previously could use it to select appropriate media for a variety of instructional situations.

Several different groups of individuals participated in the second, third, and fourth formative evaluation cycles, including Army instructional designers and university graduate students. The designers who participated in these cycles of formative evaluation worked individually with one of the developers of the model. The designers were given copies of the media selection flowchart and were asked to read instructions preceding it. Following this, they were presented with a written description of how the model would be used in a particular situation. Throughout this process, they were encouraged to make comments and ask questions.

After reading the example, each designer was given a list describing six instructional situations, and was asked to use the media selection flowchart to identify the appropriate media to employ in each case. Each situation was defined in such a way that there were only one or two correct paths to be taken through the flowchart. A record was made of deviations from the correct paths, so as to reveal possible flaws in the flowchart.

After working through all six situations, those who participated in the third and fourth evaluation cycles were asked to complete an attitude questionnaire containing 11 items of a five-point scale pertaining to the model. The questionnaire also contained a free-response section in which designers could make additional comments.

The model was revised after each group of designers completed their participation in the process. As would be expected, the number of changes that were made decreased with successive cycles. Few changes were made during the fourth cycle because participants in this cycle had very little difficulty using the model correctly.

Attitude data collected during the third and fourth evaluation cycles showed that the 11 designers participating in these stages had very positive attitudes toward the model. Ten of the 11 items on the attitude questionnaire were responded to positively by at least nine of the designers. All of the designers agreed that (a) the model included most of the important questions that should be asked when selecting media, (b) the number of questions included in the model was manageable, (c) the flowchart format was convenient to use, and (d) the model resulted in appropriate media choices. Only six of the 11 designers affirmed a high probability that the model would be used on the job. However, this finding may have been influenced by administrative restrictions on media selection procedures at one of the locations where the model was evaluated. On the whole, these results tend to confirm the achievement of the model's goal as a system easy to use and effective for the selection of appropriate media in various instructional situations.

Ways of Using the Model

The model for media selection described in this book is versatile. It can be used in the planning of a great variety of different programs of education and training. While potential users may need to ignore certain charts (Figures 3-8) that are irrelevant to their particular needs, that is a planned feature which contributes to the model's versatility. The following sections provide a general account of possible users. While some examples have been given in Chapter 1, here are some of the broader categories of situations in which media selection may occur.

1. *Public schools.* Teachers who are alert to the advantages of audio-visual media and interactive media may make learning-effective choices in designing instruction for all kinds of learning objectives in any subject. Administrative personnel of schools and school systems can use the model to advantage in choosing effective media for curricula that are already in place, or for those that may be newly adopted. A systematic procedure for choosing media is likely to be worthwhile in association with curricula from kindergarten through high school. Media specialists in schools will find the model a convenient tool for selecting media and for evaluating them, in fulfilling the purposes of a media center.
2. *Post-secondary educational institutions.* In colleges and universities, media specialists, course designers, and instructors are likely to be faced with the need to choose effective media for planned courses in a variety of subjects. The traditional media of chalkboard writing and printed text may, with appropriate planning, give way to media that add to instructional effectiveness.
3. *Organizations, private and public.* In many business organizations, from those with few employees to those with many, the training of personnel must be undertaken in order to insure the quality of the product or service to be marketed. Training can be, and often is, a substantial portion of the cost of enterprise. Properly designed and selected media can help reduce this cost. For example, the learning and practice of office-clerical skills by means of interactive media can be both an effective and efficient method of training. However, cost savings will accrue only when the training is well designed, and this means that media for the training must be properly selected with due regard for the instructional objectives. The importance of good media selection is, of course, magnified as the size of

the training activity increases. Large companies whose operations are labor-intensive have long ago recognized the value of careful media selection. Our military services likewise are highly cognizant of the value of proper media selection for the training of large numbers of personnel. In fact, military training frequently leads to employing media in innovative ways.

The model for media selection can be used as a convenient tool by those who plan programs and courses of training. In use, it enables designers of programs of education and training to eliminate from consideration those media which are not appropriate for the particular instructional objective being planned. With a smaller number of candidate media, cost-effective decisions can then be made. The model can also be used by managers of instructional programs to evaluate the appropriateness of media in existing courses of education and training. The need for revision and re-planning can be identified by such review.

What Benefits Does the Model Provide?

Some of the positively valuable characteristics of the model, as revealed by its formative evaluation and by limited observation of its use, are described briefly in the following paragraphs.

1. *Compatibility with instructional design models.* The media selection model is designed to fit with modern practice in instructional design and development. This is particularly the case for the ISD Model (Branson *et al.*, 1975), and the principles of design described by Briggs and Wager (1981), Dick and Carey (1978), and Gagné and Briggs (1979). However, compatibility extends to many other models reviewed by Andrews and Goodson (1980).

2. *Learning effectiveness focus.* The model aims at learning effectiveness, and this is the primary theme underlying its

development. A thorough-going rationale is provided for media choice, based upon events of instruction which are appropriate, according to learning theory, for five categories of learning outcomes (Gagné, 1977; Gagné and Briggs, 1979).

3. *Ease of use.* This flowchart model can be used easily and with great economy of time. The "big decisions" about training, represented by the panels of the flowchart, are removed first, so that they do not continue to introduce confusion into the media choice process. Having determined, for example, that training will be done by an instructor to students who are not competent readers, media choices are then limited to certain remaining possibilities. The designer does not have to revisit the question, "But what if the students are not good readers?" This question has already been decided, and the flowchart can be followed without hesitation. Still another circumstance favoring ease of use is the provision of step-by-step examples in Chapter 6.

4. *Defined terms.* The present model employs terms referring to media and their selection which are carefully defined. There are, first of all, definitions of media. This is considered a valuable feature, because there are many variations in common usage of names for media. For example, although the distinction between "simulator" and "training device" has been understood by builders of such equipment for many years, the distinction continues to become blurred by successive generations of trainers. When such devices are actually in use, what they are called makes little difference; when they are being built as the result of media selection, however, the difference in cost may be enormous.

Other kinds of definitions are incorporated in the new model, as described in this book. The term "medium" (or as usually employed in the plural, "media") is itself defined, helping to eliminate the confusion that sometimes creeps into procedures in instructional planning. Still another type of definition included in the present model is incorporated in the "steps" of the flowchart. Each question appearing in the flowchart is explained in detail.

5. *Media variety*. The variety of media encompassed by the present model covers a very broad range. On the one hand, the model takes care not to neglect the simplest and most readily available media such as a chalkboard, the printed page, or the instructor's voice. On the other hand, it includes the most complex and large categories of "simulator" and "real equipment." These categories, of course, simply reflect the size and complexity of equipment of the job or task for which training is designed. Variations in media brought about by modifications are also taken into account. For example, television as a medium displaying dynamic pictures accompanied by a sound track is distinguished from "interactive" television, which may be accomplished by the addition of a printed workbook and suitable provision for feedback to the student.

6. *Modifiability*. As described here, the model is viewed as distinctly modifiable. If new media or media systems are developed, the model can readily be modified by simply identifying the learning conditions they provide. The theoretical base of the model is the source of flexibility which makes possible the analysis of learning conditions that may be implied by newly developed media systems. As media options become more complex, the use of a model such as this is likely to be of increased value.

7. *Adaptability*. In situations in which media options are limited, the model indicates the appropriateness of those options. Even if none of the available media turns out to be an optimal selection, the rationale and guidelines of the model allow an instructional designer to adapt available media so as to make them most effective. The model itself, of course, may be adapted to particular circumstances of use, and clues to such changes may be obtained from the review of other selection models reviewed in Chapter 2.

8. *Practicality*. The current model provides the user with a set of media from which to choose. In most cases, any of several media may be equally appropriate so far as learning effectiveness is

concerned. Accordingly, the model avoids attempting to identify the "ideal medium" for a given situation. Following the progressive elimination of media which are inappropriate for the learning desired, the model provides a simple set of procedures for making final selection decisions based upon practical factors such as cost, availability, and convenience of use.

Research Questions

While there is evidence to indicate that the media selection model described here is a useful one, there are a number of questions concerning the value of the model that remain to be answered. Some of these are contained in the following paragraphs.

1. Does the model identify the most appropriate media to use in a given instructional situation? In answering this question, it is important to bear in mind that the media listed as appropriate for use in a particular instructional situation are included because of the conditions of learning they make possible. If two media are equally capable of providing a given set of learning conditions, then they should be able to present the same instructional message with equal learning effectiveness. In other words, as noted by Salomon and Clark (1977), if an instructional research study involves the manipulation of only the medium employed, and all other factors remain constant, no differences in learning are likely to occur as a result of that manipulation. Much of the media research conducted over the past 50 years bears witness to this conclusion (Schramm, 1977).

Learning effectiveness is determined by the conditions of learning that the medium provides. Does this mean that any medium can be used effectively in presenting a particular instructional unit? The answer is no, because not all media are equally capable of providing a given set of learning conditions.

The Model's Potential

What we have attempted to do is identify those media most capable of providing the learning conditions needed for a given instructional situation.

Two questions now arise. First, have we correctly identified the conditions of learning that should be established? And second, have we correctly identified the media capable of providing those conditions of learning? If both of these questions can be answered in the affirmative, then it is possible to state that the model does identify the appropriate media.

With regard to the first question, the learning conditions we describe have been employed as a basis for our model because previous research has identified their relevance. For example, the work of Bandura (1969) has shown that the use of human models in an instructional sequence is a highly effective condition for establishing or changing attitudes. These research findings have led us to suggest that when choosing an instructional medium that is to be used to influence learner attitudes, the ability of a medium to depict a human model should be considered.

As for the second question, we contend that the media we have identified can provide the conditions of learning that should be established in a given situation. However, other media, either used individually or in combination, may be employed in such a way as to present the necessary learning conditions. For example, computers may be suitable for teaching of attitudes, if they possess appropriate sound and graphic capabilities.

2. Are the media choices that the model specifies the same as those that "experts" would make? Undoubtedly, there are many people who are considered to be "experts" in media selection, owing either to their published work in the field, or to their experience in selecting media, or both. It would be of some interest to compare the media selection choices the model specifies with the ones that those "experts" would make. One procedure for conducting such a comparison would be to describe a series of instructional situations to a group of experts and let each one indicate the medium or media appropriate for use in that situation. The experts' choices could then be compared with the media identified as appropriate by the current model.

What would be the potential implications of the results of such a comparison? If most of the experts' choices agreed with those indicated by the model, a reasonable degree of confidence could be placed in the procedure the model prescribes. However, if most of the experts were in agreement and their choices differed from those suggested by the model, it would be most edifying to explore the reasons why the experts' choices were different. Identifying the factors the experts considered in arriving at their decisions would be an important activity. Perhaps the experts may have considered factors for which the model does not account. If this were the case, it would be wise to consider revising the model so that it makes provision for these factors.

The possibility also exists that there would be considerable disagreement among the experts. In that case, it would still be desirable to identify the factors the different experts considered in making their choices. Differences in decisions might then be accounted for, and additional factors could be identified for incorporation in the model.

3. Are the media choices that the model specifies the same as those that "non-experts" would make? In our discussion of the previous question, we indicated that agreement between the media choices suggested by the model and those suggested by media selection experts would be a positive sign. Such agreement, however, would raise a question about the usefulness of the model. If experts can arrive at appropriate media selection decisions without using the model, what purpose does the model serve?

One answer might be that the model helps "non-experts" (people who have had little or no experience in selecting media) make decisions of media selection. In order to test the validity of this notion, one might compare the choices the model proposes

The Model's Potential

with the choices non-experts make when they do not use a model. Should the choices be basically the same, the value of the model might be questioned. If the choices are essentially different, a question as to their relative merit would arise. This question could be answered by asking a group of experts to rate the two sets of choices.

4. Is the scope of instruction for which media are chosen of the appropriate size? The scope of instruction for which media are to be chosen is larger in our model than in some others. Whereas some suggest that media should be selected for individual instructional events (Branson *et al.*, 1975; Briggs and Wager, 1981; Gagné and Briggs, 1979; Gropper, 1976) or single objectives (Romiszowski, 1974; Tosti and Ball, 1969), we propose that media be selected for either a single objective or a clustered set of objectives which are part of the same lesson or module, and which belong to the same domain of learning outcomes. The question to be asked is whether working with segments smaller than those we recommend results in a better choice of media for a lesson or module. Briggs (1982) points out that research along this line could be quite fruitful, leading to the improvement of instructional design models.

In many cases, when small segments of instruction are examined, the various media identified as appropriate for individual events or objectives are collectively reviewed. Subsequently chosen is that medium, or combination of media, which appears to be most suited to the largest portion of the lesson or module. Under such a procedure, the value of selecting media for small segments of instruction is likely to be diminished when a final selection decision is made. Given this shortcoming, it appears doubtful that there are substantial advantages to the procedure of choosing media for segments of instruction smaller than those with which our model deals.

5. How useful is this model in comparison to other media selection models? A question similar to this one was asked by

Braby (1973), who conducted a study to compare the usefulness of several different media selection techniques. In that study, six instructional designers were asked to learn and use ten selection techniques. Each designer independently applied each of the ten techniques to seven training tasks. Thus, each designer made a total of 70 media selection choices. Each of these choices was then rated by two media selection experts. The ratings for all of the choices made with each technique were then summed and compared. Also compared were the designers' estimates of each technique's usefulness and the time it took for the designers to learn and apply each technique.

Many techniques for selecting media, including the one described in this book, were developed following the time of the Braby study. In order to determine the relative usefulness of these techniques, another study similar to Braby's might be undertaken.

6. Does the model account for all the important variables affecting learning effectiveness? We believe that the model accounts for the major factors of potential aid to learning. However, as additional research on human learning is conducted, new principles that should be incorporated into the model are likely to be discovered. Although of limited usefulness as yet, two types of research studies show promise of being of particular value in the formation of media selection principles. These are studies of media attributes (Levie and Dickie, 1973), and aptitude-treatment interaction studies (Cronbach and Snow, 1977; Salomon, 1979).

7. Is the model compatible with other theories of learning and communication? Many of the principles incorporated in our model were derived from cognitive learning theory, as it is described in such works as the *Handbook*, edited by Estes (1975, 1976, 1978), and volumes by Anderson (1980), and Bower and Hilgard (1981). The model, however, is also compatible with the principles of behavioristic views of learning. Behavioral learning theory posits that learners should practice correct responses and receive reinforcement for doing so. These principles are accounted for in our model.

The Model's Potential

The model is not incompatible with the work of Salomon (1979) on the cultivation of learner abilities. Although the symbol systems he identifies go beyond the characteristics of media we employ, the latter properties serve to distinguish what are called "technological attributes." Should the cultivation of cognitive skills become a practical reality, modification of the present model would need to begin with the addition of these instructional objectives.

The correspondence of ideas in our model and those of theories of learning and communication should be readily possible to determine. This kind of comparison may be undertaken by examining the principles of such theories against those principles that form the basis for our model, as described in Chapter 3.

Concluding Statement

The model of media selection described in this volume is based upon principles derived from learning research and theory. Its initial formulation was subjected to four cycles of formative evaluation and revision. These tryouts were carried out with people knowledgeable about the design of instruction and media selection, including military training designers (the users originally intended).

A number of uses for the model can be identified, in schools and in other organizations having educational missions. Positive features of the model for these various using agencies include its (1) compatibility with instructional design procedures; (2) focus on learning effectiveness; (3) ease of use; (4) employment of defined terms; and (5) provision for media variety. In addition, it is noted that the model can be readily modified, is adaptable to local requirements, and leads to practical decisions. Research questions that appear worth pursuing in connection with the model's use are those providing comparisons with other models, with judgments of experts and non-experts, and the compatibility of media choice decisions with theories of learning and communication.

References

Anderson, J.R. *Cognitive psychology and its implications.* San Francisco: Freeman, 1980.

Andrews, D., and Goodson, L. A comparative analysis of models of instructional design. *Journal of Instructional Development,* 1980, *3*(4), 2-16.

Bandura, A. *Principles of behavior modification.* New York: Holt, Rinehart, and Winston, 1969.

Bower, G.H., and Hilgard, E.J. *Theories of learning* (5th ed.). Englewood Cliffs, NJ: Prentice-Hall, 1981.

Braby, R. *An evaluation of ten techniques for choosing instructional media* (TAEG Report No. 8). Orlando, FL: Training Analysis and Evaluation Group, 1973.

Branson, R.K., Rayner, G.T., Cox, J.L., Furman, J.P., King, F.J., and Hannum, W.H. *Interservice procedures for instructional systems development* (5 vols.) (TRADOC Pam 350-30). Ft. Monroe, VA: U.S. Army Training and Doctrine Command, August 1975.

Briggs, L.J. Instructional design: Present strengths and limitations, and a view of the future. *Educational Technology,* 1982, *22*(10), 18-23.

Briggs, L.J., and Wager, W.W. *Handbook of procedures for the design of instruction* (2nd ed.). Englewood Cliffs, NJ: Educational Technology Publications, 1981.

Cronbach, L.J., and Snow, R.E. *Aptitudes and instructional methods.* New York: Irvington, 1977.

Dick, W., and Carey, L. *The systematic design of instruction.* Glenview, IL: Scott, Foresman, 1978.

Estes, W.K. (Ed.) *Handbook of learning and cognitive processes, Vol. 1: Introduction to concepts and issues.* Hillsdale, NJ: Erlbaum, 1975.

Estes, W.K. *Handbook of learning and cognitive processes, Vol. 4: Attention and memory.* Hillsdale, NJ: Erlbaum, 1976.

Estes, W.K. *Handbook of learning and cognitive processes, Vol. 5: Human information processing.* Hillsdale, NJ: Erlbaum, 1978.

Gagné, R.M. *The conditions of learning* (3rd ed.). New York: Holt, Rinehart, and Winston, 1977.

Gagné, R.M., and Briggs, L.J. *Principles of instructional design* (2nd ed.). New York: Holt, Rinehart, and Winston, 1979.

Gropper, G.L. A behavioral perspective on media selection. *AV Communication Review*, 1976, *24*, 157-186.

Levie, W.H., and Dickie, K.E. The analysis and application of media. In R.M.W. Travers (Ed.), *Second handbook of research on teaching.* Chicago: Rand McNally, 1973.

Romiszowski, A.J. *The selection and use of instructional media.* London: Kogan Page, 1974.

Salomon, G. *Interaction of media, cognition, and learning.* San Francisco: Jossey-Bass, 1979.

Salomon, G., and Clark, R.E. Media research methodology. *Review of Educational Research*, 1977, *47*, 99-120.

Schramm, W. *Big media, little media.* Beverly Hills, CA: Sage, 1977.

Tosti, D.T., and Ball, J.R. A behavioral approach to instructional design and media selection. *AV Communication Review*, 1969, *17*, 5-25.

Index

Age of learners, as a media selection factor, 16, 20-21
Anderson, J.R., 36, 46, 118, 120
Anderson, R.H., 12, 15, 16, 17, 18, 21, 27, 36, 46
Andrews, D., 111, 120
Angert, J.F., 4, 9
Association for Educational Communications and Technology, 18, 27
Atkinson, R.C., 55, 64
Attitudes, 40, 72-74, 75
 appropriate media, 40, 75
Audio capability of media, as a media selection factor, 16-17
Audio media, 62-63

Ball, J.R., 12, 14, 15, 16, 17, 20, 22, 23, 28, 36, 47, 117, 121
Bandura, A., 40, 46, 57, 64, 75, 84, 115, 120
Bower, G.H., 36, 42, 46, 118, 120
Braby, R., 11, 27, 118, 120
Bracht, G.H., 20, 27
Bransford, J.D., 38, 46
Branson, R.K., 12, 13, 15, 16, 17, 18, 20, 21, 22, 27, 111, 117, 120
Bretz, R., 12, 15, 16, 17, 19, 20, 22, 23, 24, 25, 27, 36, 46
Briggs, L.J., 11, 12, 13, 14, 15, 16, 17, 18, 20, 21, 22, 23, 24, 27, 28, 36, 37, 41, 47, 61, 64, 111, 112, 117, 120, 121
Bruner, J.S., 44, 47

Campeau, P.L., 61, 64
Carey, L., 111, 120
Central broadcast, decision to use, 72
Chalkboard, 49, 59
Charts, 49, 59
Chu, G.C., 6, 9
Clark, F.E., 4, 9
Clark, R.E., 114, 121
Cognitive strategies, 39
 appropriate media, 39
Color capability of media, as a selection factor, 18
Computers, 54-55
Cone of Experience, 21
Cox, J.L., 12, 27, 120
Cronbach, L.J., 20, 28, 118, 120

Dale, E.A., 19, 21, 28, 36, 46
Dick, W., 111, 120
Dickie, K.E., 118, 121
Dwyer, F.M., 18, 19, 28

Estes, W.K., 36, 43, 46, 118, 121
Events of instruction (see Instructional events)
Experience of learners, as a media selection factor, 20-21, 43-44

Filmstrips, 58
Fitts, P.M., 39, 47
Friend, J., 38, 47, 52, 65
Furman, J.P., 12, 27, 120

Gage, N.L., 63, 65

123

Gagné, R.M., 6-7, 9, 11n., 12, 13, 15, 16, 17, 20, 21, 22, 23, 24, 28, 32, 36, 37, 41, 43, 47, 61, 64, 65, 74, 75, 84, 111, 112, 117, 121
Games, 50-51
Goodson, L., 111, 120
Gropper, G.L., 12, 14, 15, 21, 22, 23, 24, 28, 117, 121

Hannum, W.H., 12, 27, 120
Hardware, definition of, 5
Heidt, E.U., 12, 18, 28
Heinich, R., 19, 28
Hilgard, E.J., 36, 46, 118, 120
Hornik, R.C., 52, 65
Human model, 40

Instructional designers, use of systematic media selection procedures by, 7
Instructional events
  as a media selection factor, 5-6, 22-25, 41, 43
  assessing performance
    appropriate media for, 24-25
    purpose of, 24
  defined, 22, 37, 41
  eliciting performance
    appropriate media for, 23-24, 42-43
    purpose of, 23, 42-43
  enhancing retention and transfer
    appropriate media for, 43
    purpose of, 43
  informing learners of objectives
    appropriate media for, 22-23
    purpose of, 22-23
  order in which they occur, 41
  presenting stimulus materials
    appropriate media for, 23, 42
    purpose of, 23, 42
  providing feedback
    appropriate media for, 24, 43
    purpose of, 24, 42-43
  providing learning guidance
    appropriate media for, 42
    purpose of, 42
  theoretical derivation of, 41
Instructional setting
  as a media selection factor, 18, 19-20, 26-27
  defined, 19
Instructors, as media, 63-64
Intellectual skills, 37-38, 74
  appropriate media, 38, 74
Interactive media
  examples of, 38, 39, 53, 54, 55-56
  need for, 38, 39-40, 43

Kemp, J.E., 12, 14, 15, 16, 17, 18, 28, 36, 47
King, F.J., 12, 27, 120

Large equipment, 49-51
Learner abilities, cultivation of, 44, 119
Learner characteristics, as a media selection factor, 16, 17, 20-21, 24-25, 26-27, 43-44
Learning outcomes
  as a media selection factor, 21-22, 26-27, 38-40
  categories of, 21, 37-40
Lesser, G.S., 52, 65
Levie, W.H., 12, 28, 118, 121

May, M.A., 61, 64
Mayo, J.K., 52, 65
McAnany, E.G., 52, 65
Media
  categories of, 13-14, 49
  definition of instructional, 5
  description of types of, 49-64
Media attributes, as a media selection factor, 14-19, 26-27

Index

Media research, 6-7, 114
Media selection
  importance of, 3-4
  when it should take place, 5
Media selection models—model developed by Reiser and Gagné
  adaptability of, 113
  appropriateness of model's media choices, 114-115
  attitudes toward, 109
  audience for whom model is intended, 7-8, 109-111
  basis in learning research and theory, 36-44
  benefits of, 31, 45, 109, 111-114, 119
  bottom-line boxes, 35-36
  candidate media, definition of, 31
  characteristics of, 4-5, 16, 31-32, 44-45, 105, 111-114
  charts (see flowchart, panels)
  comparisons between model's media choices and "expert" opinion, 115-116
  comparisons between model's media choices and "non-expert" opinion, 116-117
  comparisons with other models, 117-118
  compatibility with instructional design models, 111
  compatibility with theories of learning and communication, 118-119
  ease of use, 31, 45, 112
  examples of use of, 85-104
  factors considered in, 4-5, 16, 45, 67-84, 105, 111-112, 118
  final selection procedure
    description of, 82-84
    examples of, 88, 94, 97-99, 100, 103
  flowchart
    examples of use of, 87-103
    how to use, 33-36, 67-84
    information needed prior to using, description of, 32-33, 67-68
    information needed prior to using, examples of, 87, 89, 95, 99, 102
    panels, 31-32, 33-35, 70-82
    questions, explanation of, 33-35, 70-82
  formative evaluation of, 107-109
  learning effectiveness, model's focus upon, 45, 111-112, 118
  media selection worksheet
    examples of use of, 87-89, 91-104
    how to use, 68, 82-83
  modifiability of, 113
  practicality of, 113-114
  research questions, 114-120
  scope of instruction for which media are chosen, 68, 117
Media selection models—other models
  applicability of, 3
  characteristics of, 4, 12-27
  factors considered in, 4, 14-27
  formats used, 12-13, 26
  research on, 11
Molenda, M., 19, 28
Morningstar, M., 55, 65
Motion capability of media, as a selection factor, 17-18
Motion pictures, with sound, 56-57
Motor skills, 39-40, 74, 78
  appropriate media, 39-40, 74, 78

Nugent, G.C., 57, 65

Olson, D.R., 44, 47
O'Neil, H.F., 39, 47
Overhead projections, 60-61

Paivio, A., 42, 47
Portable equipment, 49-51
Posner, M.I., 40, 47
Practical factors
  examples of, 25-26
    role in media selection, 25-26, 27
Print capability of media, as a selection factor, 16-17
Printed text, 61-62
Programmed text, 61-62

Radio, broadcast, 51-52
Rayner, G.T., 12, 27, 120
Reading ability of learners, as a media selection factor, 16, 17, 20, 24-25, 44, 78
Real equipment, 18-19, 49-51
Real objects (see Real equipment)
Reiser, R.A., 7, 9, 11n.
Romiszowski, A.J., 11, 12, 15, 16, 17, 18, 21, 22, 23, 28, 36, 47, 117, 121
Russell, J.D., 19, 28

Salomon, G., 19, 28, 44, 47, 114, 118, 119, 121
Schramm, W., 3, 6, 7, 9, 18, 28, 51, 65, 114, 121
Searle, B., 38, 47, 52, 65
Self-instruction, 76-80
Simulation, 50-51
Simulators, 50-51
Slides, 60-61
Slide/tape, 58
Snow, R.E., 20, 28, 118, 120
Sound capability of media (see Audio capability of media)
Sound media (see Audio media)
Suppes, P., 38, 47, 52, 55, 65

Task error, consequences of
  as a media selection factor, 49-51, 70-72

explanation of concept, 70, 87
Television, broadcast, 51-52
Television, interactive, 55-56
Tosti, D.T., 12, 14, 15, 16, 17, 20, 22, 23, 28, 36, 47, 117, 121
Training aids, 59
Training Analysis and Evaluation Group, 11, 28
Training devices, 53-54
TV cassettes, 56-57

Verbal information, 38-39, 72-74, 75
  appropriate media, 39
Visual capability of media, as a selection factor, 16, 74-76

Wager, W.W., 12, 13, 14, 15, 16, 17, 18, 20, 21, 22, 28, 111, 117, 120
Winn, W., 19, 28